GWENDOLYN LEE

About the Author

ANDREW SHAFFER is the founder and creative director of Order of St. Nick, the greeting card company whose irreverent cards have been featured on *The Colbert Report*, NPR, and FOX News. He has a graduate degree from the University of Iowa, where he also attended the Iowa Writers' Workshop for a summer semester. He lives in Iowa with his wife. Visit him online at www.orderofstandrew.com.

reat philosophers who failed at love   andrew shaffer

great philosophers
who failed
at love

great philosophers
who failed
at love

andrew shaffer

HARPER ● PERENNIAL

NEW YORK ● LONDON ● TORONTO ● SYDNEY ● NEW DELHI ● AUCKLAND

HARPER ● PERENNIAL

GREAT PHILOSOPHERS WHO FAILED AT LOVE. Copyright © 2011
by Andrew Shaffer. All rights reserved. Printed in the United States
of America. No part of this book may be used or reproduced in any
manner whatsoever without written permission except in the case of brief
quotations embodied in critical articles and reviews. For information,
address HarperCollins Publishers, 10 East 53rd Street, New York,
NY 10022.

HarperCollins books may be purchased for educational, business, or
sales promotional use. For information, please write: Special Markets
Department, HarperCollins Publishers, 10 East 53rd Street, New York,
NY 10022.

FIRST EDITION

Library of Congress Cataloging-in-Publication Data is available upon
request.

ISBN 978-0-06-196981-2

11 12 13 14 15   OV/RRD   10 9 8 7 6 5 4 3 2 1

Contents

Introduction

"It's always nice to know that no matter how badly you've screwed up your love life, someone else has done far, far worse."

—Neal Pollack

We all have questions about love; we all want to know the secrets to a successful relationship. Is she "the one"? Is it okay to date my boss? How do I know if my husband is cheating? It seems intuitive that we should look to wise men and women for the answers.

Philosophers have contemplated the most vexing questions, from ethics to politics to the very nature of being. If anyone can teach us about a concept as abstract as love, philosophers—the original "lovers of wisdom"*—should be at the top of the list.

---

* Literally: The word "philosophy" comes from the ancient Greek word *philosophia*, a composite of *philein* ("to love") and *sophia* ("wisdom").

But a lover of wisdom and a wise lover are, as it turns out, two very different things.

While most of us have struck out at love before, the tales of many philosophers' romantic hardships and indiscretions take the wedding cake. You might have forgotten an anniversary, but at least you didn't strangle your wife (Louis Althusser), adopt your mistress as your daughter (Jean-Paul Sartre), or get exiled to another country for having an affair (Seneca the Younger).

The great Western philosophers—the men and women whose intellectual acrobatics are praised by professors in Philosophy 101 courses everywhere—have consistently sabotaged their own relationships with their neurotic tendencies. In or out of love, philosophers are overly critical, condescending, and holier-than-thou. Their theories are impenetrable, their positions contradictory, their probing questions a nuisance. Such temperamental behavior has made philosophers unsuitable candidates for marriage. It is not surprising that so many philosophers simply opted out of the love game altogether.

While far too many philosophers died miserable, bitter, and alone, a few did make it through their failures to have happy marriages. Like Albert Camus, whose life was cut short by a tragic car accident *before* his wife could discover the mistresses that he had hidden around the globe. Or Henry Ward Beecher, the infamous nineteenth century adulterer, whose wife was too busy raising their ten children to even give a thought to divorcing him. Or Bertrand Russell, who found that, at least when it comes to matrimony, the *fourth* time is the charm.

The truth is that this book contains just a sampling of the thousands of great minds who have failed at love. In every era of history, big brains and broken hearts have gone hand in hand, and the bigger they come, the harder they fail. Perhaps Bob Dylan was the wisest of all when he admitted: "You can't be in love and wise at the same time."

philosophers

Peter Abelard
(1079–1142)

*"Let no lover hereafter follow my
example, for a woman rejected
is an outrageous creature."*

By his own estimation, French scholar Peter Abelard "confounded all the learned of the age" with his philosophical musings. At the height of his fame, after defeating his teachers in logical arguments and founding his own school, Abelard accepted the chair of the Notre Dame cathedral school in Paris in 1115. His lectures on Greek philosophy and Christian theology drew thousands of students, but seventeen-year-old Héloïse d'Argenteuil stood out from the crowd. "I saw her, I loved her, I resolved to make her love me," Abelard reflected in his autobiography.

Héloïse lived with her uncle Fulbert, a canon of the cathedral—not a man to be trifled with. This presented only a minor challenge for Abelard, who devised a plan to steal Héloïse out from under the canon's watchful eye. "I was ambitious in my choice [of lady], and wished to find some obstacles, that I might surmount them with the greater glory and pleasure," Abelard wrote. He befriended Fulbert through a mutual acquaintance, and in a stroke of luck, Fulbert hired him to educate Héloïse in philosophy. "Can you believe it, he allowed me the privilege of his table, and an apartment in his house? [And] by this means

I found opportunities of being in private with her," Abelard wrote, clearly pleased with himself.

Héloïse fell in love with her mentor, who was over twice her age; their private tutoring sessions quickly degenerated into lessons of the flesh. Soon their love couldn't be contained to daylight hours, and they secretly met at night to "express mutual affections." As one of Abelard's contemporaries put it bluntly, the learned professor "taught her not to argue but to fornicate." Rumors of Abelard and Héloïse's affair spread throughout Paris, eventually circling back to Fulbert's ears. The enraged uncle tossed the professor out of his home and onto the street.

Abelard refused to abandon his young lover. After renting an apartment near Fulbert's house, he met with Héloïse's maid Agaton. He asked her to be an intermediary between himself and Héloïse. Unfortunately for Abelard, the maid had her own feelings for him:

> I am in love with you, Abelard; I know you adore Héloïse, and I do not blame you; I desire only to enjoy the second place in your affections. Do not perplex yourself with scruples; a prudent man should love several at the same time, then if one should fail he is not left unprovided.

Sounds like a sensible proposal, no? But not to Abelard, whose heart belonged to but one woman. He shot down Agaton's advances, and the spurned maid vengefully exposed Abelard's continued pursuit of Héloïse to Fulbert. "A woman rejected is an outrageous creature," Abelard wrote of the maid's tattling.

Agaton's report threw Héloïse's uncle into a fit of rage, rendering futile any attempt by Abelard to get back into his good graces. It seemed that the lovers had never been further apart. To complicate matters, Héloïse was pregnant.

Abelard, at the end of his rope, did the only sensible thing: He scaled the walls of Fulbert's house, abducted Héloïse in a daring rescue, and whisked her away in the dead of night. He hid her away in his hometown of Brittany, where she gave birth to their love child.*

Abelard, fearing a public scandal, began to have second thoughts—perhaps he had acted too hastily. Determined to ease tensions with her uncle, he proposed to marry Héloïse. Astonishingly, Fulbert accepted the peace offering, and Abelard and Héloïse were wed in a secret ceremony.

Héloïse was against their marriage, believing it to be no more than a business transaction that would drain their relationship of its natural passion. "Will it not be more agreeable to me

---

* Their only child, Astralabe, was named after the astrolabe, an astronomical instrument popular in the twelfth century. Not only did both of Astralabe's parents abandon him to his aunt, they also made it nearly impossible to pronounce his name without being reminded of a discrete part of the female anatomy. This particular problem was confounded when the Latin spelling of his name was used: *Astralabius*.

to see myself your mistress than your wife?" she said, adding that "the cries of children and the cares of a family [are] utterly inconsistent with the tranquility which study require." This was partially true—Abelard *had* been neglecting his philosophical studies while playing house. He reluctantly consented to his wife's demands and shipped her off to a convent for safekeeping. Their son ended up in the care of Héloïse's sister.

What occurred next was an event that historians have delicately described as "a certain well enough known event when [Abelard] was not well treated." When Fulbert found out that his niece had been sent away to the convent, he had Abelard castrated. With chilling detachment, Abelard wrote:

> An assassin came into my bedchamber by night, with a
> razor in his hand, and found me in a deep sleep. I suf-
> fered the most shameful punishment that the revenge of
> an enemy could invent; in short, without losing my life,
> I lost my manhood.

In one of the most remarkable examples of positive thinking ever recorded, Abelard envisioned the castration as a liberation from his past debauchery. He found solace in a monastery, where he was finally able to write to his heart's content. "I [found] in philosophy and religion a remedy for my disgrace; I searched out an asylum to secure me from love."

Héloïse wrote often to her estranged husband, and their

amorous exchanges have become a legend in their own right. "I cannot live if you will not tell me that you still love me," she wrote in one letter, adding that she loved him as a person and not as a man—castration be damned.

As their correspondence progressed over the years, Abelard's tone transformed from that of a lover to that of a priest. In one of his final letters to Héloïse, he urged her to devote herself to Christ and forget about her wounded lover: "You will hereafter apply yourself in good earnest to the business of your salvation; this ought to be your whole concern. Banish me, therefore, forever from your heart."

Abelard continued his studies, eventually founding the Abbey of the Paraclete monastery. Héloïse, however, refused to banish Abelard from her heart. She outlived him by twenty-two years and is buried beside him in the abbey's graveyard.

IN HIS OWN WORDS
We Make a Great Couplet

Abelard's clandestine love affair with his student wreaked havoc upon his own study habits. Instead of reading and writing philosophy, he devoted his time to composing amorous poetry. Amazingly, he proved to be a poet of unusual talent. By simply reciting Abelard's poetry, young men were able to obtain "favors" from young ladies. As the part-time laureate explained, "Those who were in love as I was took a pride in learning [my poems], and by luckily applying my thoughts and verses they obtained favors which perhaps they would not otherwise have gained." Fortunately for chaste young ladies everywhere, his poetry is long since lost.

Louis Althusser
(1918–1990)

*"The trouble is, there are bodies and,
worse still, sexual organs."*

Louis Althusser was a thirty-year-old virgin when he met the thirty-eight-year-old Hélène Rytman. The older woman introduced the French philosopher to a brave new sexual world, a world that Althusser may not have been ready for: After sleeping with Hélène for the first time, Althusser was so mentally disturbed that he fell into a deep depression, requiring shock treatment and hospitalization. Despite the bad omens, Althusser eventually accepted sex as part of his life and married Hélène.

In fact, Hélène may have taught her young lover too well; he quickly began cheating on her with other women. Their marriage was punctuated by violent fights, and Hélène frequently threatened to kill herself. That they had no close friends only compounded their marital woes. None of this helped Althusser's fragile mental state, and he required frequent hospitalizations and extensive psychoanalytic treatments.

Astonishingly, Althusser was still able to teach throughout his troubles. He lectured for more than thirty years at the École Normale Supérieure in Paris, influencing an entire generation of French thinkers with his radical Marxist philosophy.

Althusser's life came crashing down on him when, in the

early hours of a quiet Sunday morning in 1980, he "accidentally" murdered his wife. As Althusser wrote with disturbing clarity:

> Kneeling beside her, leaning across her body, I was massaging her neck. I would often silently massage the nape of her neck and her back. . . .
>
> But on this occasion I was massaging the front of her neck. . . .
>
> Hélène's face was calm and motionless; her eyes were open and staring at the ceiling.
>
> Suddenly, I was terror-struck. Her eyes stared interminably, and I noticed the tip of her tongue was showing between her teeth and lips, strange and still.
>
> I had seen dead bodies before, of course, but never in my life looked into the face of someone who had been strangled. Yet I knew she had been strangled. But how? I stood up and screamed: "I've strangled Hélène!"

He claimed that he was suffering from an acute state of mental confusion stemming from years of manic depression. He was subsequently judged mentally unfit to stand trial and spent almost three years institutionalized in psychiatric hospitals before being released back into society in 1982. He lived in and out of hospitals until his death eight years later, somehow finding the time and sanity to complete his autobiography, *The Future Lasts Forever*.

IN HIS OWN WORDS
Surprise!

"I have also, I think, learnt what it is to love. . . . Being thoughtful in relation to others, respecting their desires, their rhythms, never demanding things but learning to receive and to accept every gift as a surprise, and being capable, in a wholly unassuming way, of giving and of surprising the other person, without the least coercion," Althusser wrote. His wife was undoubtedly surprised when she woke to find herself being strangled to death by her own husband.

Saint Thomas Aquinas
(1225–1274)

"Love takes up where knowledge leaves off."

Thomas Aquinas was not an average teenage rebel. At age seventeen, he ran away from his Italian home . . . to join a religious order.

His family wanted him to become a Benedictine monk; Aquinas wanted to join the Order of St. Dominic, a rival Christian faction. While he was en route to the Order of St. Dominic in Rome, two of his brothers kidnapped him and locked him in a cell at the Castle of Monte San Giovanni, an imposing fortress that doubled as his father's home. If anything could break young Aquinas's faith, his family reasoned, it would be lockdown in a castle.

Despite being imprisoned, Aquinas refused to renounce his devotion to the Dominicans. In a desperate ploy, his family hired a prostitute to seduce him. They prayed that once Aquinas had sinned with the woman he would give up his clerical aspirations.

Recognizing the woman's amorous intentions the moment she was thrown into his cell, Aquinas drove her away with a hot firebrand. He begged God for the strength to carry on in the face of further temptations of the flesh.

That night, God answered him in the form of two angels.

While the angels did not help him escape, they did him one better: They tied a white cord about his waist. "Thomas, on God's behalf, we gird you with the cincture of chastity, which no attack will ever destroy," the angels sang in harmony. With the power bestowed upon his loins by the magical rope, Aquinas was able to endure his captivity with a renewed sense of faith.

Finally, after two years of imprisonment, Aquinas escaped; his family made no attempts to recapture him. He joined the Order of St. Dominic and became a priest of the Roman Catholic Church.

Today, Aquinas is widely considered the greatest Catholic theologian. And that rope tied around his waist? Aquinas wore it until his death and bragged that he was never tempted to break his vow of chastity.*

IN HIS OWN WORDS
For Unlawful Carnal Knowledge

Aquinas believed that some sins, such as adultery, are punishable on both physical and spiritual levels. Adultery "is not only

---

* This is suspiciously reminiscent of the technique that farmers use to castrate sheep: A strong rubber band is fastened around a ram's testicles to cut off circulation, and the animal is allowed to run free until its jewels eventually drop off due to necrosis.

the fleshly sin of lust, but the spiritual sin of injustice, and that of a graver sort than simple theft," Aquinas wrote in his *Summary of Theology*. He was obviously unaware of the legal concept of double jeopardy, which forbids being tried more than once for the same infraction.

Aristotle
(384–322 BC)

"How doth love show its greatest force, by making the fool to become wise, or the wise become a fool."

A ristotle has taken plenty of abuse over the years for his misogynistic views. The Greek philosopher believed that women are inherently defective creatures, based in part upon his erroneous observations that females have colder blood, fewer teeth, and shorter lives than men.* To Aristotle, women were "monstrosities" of nature and little more than tamed animals.

Many historians simply ignore his views of women. After all, he was, along with Plato and Socrates (pages 120 and 152), one of the founding fathers of Western philosophy. Aristotle created the first formal study of logic and advanced the fields of biology, ethics, and politics.

When he was thirty-seven, Aristotle married eighteen-year-old Pythias, adoptive daughter of his mentor Hermias. Their ages corresponded exactly with the optimal ages to marry, Aristotle romantically pointed out. The historical record

---

* Greeks had a curious habit of leaving unwanted female newborns outside to die of exposure. This may have skewed the average life expectancy of women in Greek society.

indicates that their marriage was a happy one. If his wife had been allowed to record her own thoughts on their relationship, a different picture may very well have emerged: Did she really enjoy being treated as a "tamed animal" and called a "monstrosity"? Pythias died at an early age, leaving Aristotle to raise their only child, a daughter also named Pythias.

Aristotle next married a woman with the unbecoming name of Herpyllis. Few details of their relationship remain, and when Aristotle died, he requested that he be buried beside his first wife. He continued to treat women like livestock to the very end: He left Herpyllis to the executors of his estate, with explicit instructions in his will that "she be given to one not unworthy" if she wished to remarry.

IN HIS OWN WORDS
Of Mouths and Men

Critics have ridiculed Aristotle for centuries for his belief that women have fewer teeth than men. "Although he was twice married, it never occurred to him to verify this statement by examining his wives' mouths," philosopher Bertrand Russell (page 134) wrote.

Perhaps he was too busy with his work to find time to check? According to Diogenes the Cynic (page 72), Aristotle "would walk up and down [a public walkway in the Lyceum] discussing philosophy with his pupils until it was time to rub themselves with oil." Women were confined to the home and barred from public and social functions, while Greek men were free to teach, learn, and rub each other down.

Saint Augustine of Hippo
(354–430)

"Give me chastity and continence, but not yet."

When Augustine left his North African home at the age of sixteen to study in Carthage (an ancient city in present-day Tunisia), he partied as if he was the first student to ever discover wine, women, and song. He neglected his homework to instead focus on "hellish pleasures," the most documented of which was a sexual relationship with a young woman whose name is unknown to us today. He wrote:

> It was a sweet thing to me both to love and to be loved, and more sweet still when I was able to enjoy the body of my lover. And so I muddied the clear spring of friendship with the dirt of physical desire and clouded over its brightness with the dark hell of lust.

Augustine remained together with the unnamed woman for thirteen years. They had a son, Adeodatus, and Augustine supported his makeshift family by teaching rhetoric. They lived a quiet, simple life, but Augustine's mother had bigger dreams for her son.

As Augustine approached thirty, his mother pressured

him to marry a "respectable woman" (i.e., not the kind of girl who would have a child out of wedlock). The woman whom he lived with—the love of his life, by his own accord—left town at Augustine's behest. Although he retained custody of their son, Augustine was nevertheless devastated. "My heart, which clung to her, was broken and wounded, and dripping blood," he wrote.

The new "respectable woman" his mother set him up with was only ten years old; she would be ineligible to marry for another two years. Augustine needed to sate his appetite for female companionship in the meantime, yet his former lover was now a continent away, exiled to Africa. He had no reservations about moving on: The man whose heart was "broken and wounded, and dripping blood" decided to take a mistress. As he later recalled, he was "in love with being in love."

Before he could be married, and while he was still seeing his new mistress, Augustine had an honest-to-God divine intervention that would forever change his life.

One day, while hanging out with a friend, a mysterious voice in his head shouted at him, "Augustine! Augustine! Take up the Bible and read!" He happened to have just such a Good Book handy. He picked it up. The first passage that he read was Romans 13:13–14:

Take part not in revelry and drunkenness, not in debauchery and licentiousness, not in quarreling and jeal-

ousy. But put on the Lord Jesus Christ, and make no
provision for the flesh, to gratify its desires.

After reading this passage, Augustine committed himself to
a life of celibacy, abandoning both his mistress and his fiancée in
the process. He converted to Catholicism and became a priest in
Hippo Regius (now an Algerian city called Annaba).

He confronted his past lasciviousness in his groundbreaking
autobiography *Confessions*. Augustine's frank recollections of
his premarital sexual experiences were considered revolutionary at the time, but he had more in mind than mere titillation. "I
intend to remind myself of my past foulnesses and carnal cor-
ruptions, not because I love them but so that I may love you, my
God," he wrote.

Augustine of Hippo would go on to write more than a hundred books, shaping the development of Western thinking with
his biblical interpretations of marriage and sexuality.

IN HIS OWN WORDS
Can't Live with 'Em, Can't Live without 'Em

Unlike many other theologians, Augustine was able to draw
upon his own precelibate experiences when writing about sexuality. He understood, for instance, that men's sexual organs had

minds of their own; the penis may become erect at inopportune moments or fail to rise to the occasion. "At times, without intention, the body stirs on its own, insistent. At other times, it leaves a straining lover in the lurch, and while desire sizzles in the imagination, it is frozen in the flesh," he wrote in *City of God*.

Simone de Beauvoir
(1908–1986)

"To catch a husband is an art; to hold him is a job."

Even as a teenager, French philosopher Simone de Beauvoir knew that she was different than other women. "I can't get rid of this idea that I am alone, in a world apart, being present at the other as at a spectacle," she wrote.

When she went to secondary school to study philosophy, her otherness was more pronounced: Beauvoir smoke and drank like a man. She attracted the attention of a fellow student, René Maheu, and wrote in her diary that the good-looking and intelligent Maheu was her "greatest happiness." Maheu nicknamed her *le castor*, French for "the Beaver." He was perfect for her in every way except one: He was married.

Meanwhile, she studied for her teaching exam with Maheu's friend Jean-Paul Sartre (page 138). Sartre was an ugly duckling, but a charming conversationalist compared to the handsome yet dull Maheu. Beauvoir and Sartre studied and talked day and night for weeks. She finished in second place on the exam; he finished first (although it was his second attempt after failing the year prior). The more time that Beauvoir spent with Sartre, the less she thought about Maheu. To her astonishment, she found herself in love with the funny-looking man. It was the beginning of the unconventional fifty-one-year relationship that would dominate Beauvoir's life and threaten to overshadow her work.

Although they often referred to each other as husband and wife in letters, Beauvoir and Sartre never married—marriage was a dirty word to the free-thinking Sartre. Beauvoir was conflicted at first; she had always imagined herself as a wife and mother. Instead, Sartre proposed an open arrangement wherein their relationship with each other would be "essential" and all others secondary. Beauvoir and Sartre lived together only sporadically and thus had plenty of time for extracurricular activities both sexual and intellectual.

In the 1950s, Beauvoir wrote the influential feminist polemic *The Second Sex*. She was also a gifted novelist and memoirist, establishing herself as a philosopher independent of Sartre. At his urging, they disclosed their sexual affairs to each other. Two collections of letters, published after both of their deaths, revealed their promiscuity: Beauvoir recounted her same-sex liaisons in tantalizing detail for Sartre, while he wrote to her about taking young girls' virginity with clinical precision. Occasionally, they pursued the same women—frequently with disturbing duplicity, comparing notes behind their conquests' backs.

Beauvoir's most passionate relationship was not with Sartre, but with American author Nelson Algren. They first met in February 1947 while Beauvoir was visiting Chicago. Algren gave her a ring and asked her to move to America to be with him. "I'm ready to marry you this very moment," he said.

Beauvoir, though deeply in love with Algren, was still under Sartre's thumb. "I could not love you, want you, and miss you more than I do," she wrote to Algren from France. "[But] for nearly twenty years [Sartre] did everything for me; he helped me to live, to find myself, he sacrificed lots of things for my sake. . . . I could not desert him [and] pledge my whole life to anyone else."

Algren grudgingly accepted her explanation and continued to see Beauvoir when they could find the time and means to rendezvous, unaware that she was still sleeping with Sartre (among others). Algren was understandably infuriated when he read an extract from Beauvoir's memoir *Force of Circumstance* in which she called her relationship with Algren a "passing sexual liaison." Algren wrote a scathing review of her book in *Harper's*. "[Pimps] are more honest than philosophers," he quipped, driving the nail into the coffin of their relationship. Still, she wore the ring that he had given her until her death.

Meanwhile, Sartre adopted his Algerian mistress, Arlette Elkaïm, as his daughter in 1965. Neither he nor Beauvoir ever had any children of their own, and the adoption was a legal necessity to ensure the sanctity of his literary legacy. Elkaïm was named the executor of Sartre's estate upon his death in 1980. Not to be outdone, Beauvoir adopted one of her own lovers,

Sylvie Le Bon, as her daughter after Sartre passed away—and named Le Bon the executor of *her* estate.

Despite the uncommon nature of their romance, Beauvoir and Sartre are forever linked by virtue of being buried together in a shared grave in Paris. "There is one thing that hasn't changed and cannot change: that is that no matter what happens and what I become, I will become it with you," Sartre once wrote to Beauvoir. "The comradeship that welded our lives together made a superfluous mockery of any other bond we might have forged for ourselves," Beauvoir said.

IN HER OWN WORDS
Separate but Equal

"There will always be certain differences between man and woman; her eroticism, and therefore her sexual world, have a special form of their own and therefore cannot fail to engender a sensuality, a sensitivity, of a special nature. This means that her relations to her own body, to that of the male, to the child, will never be identical with those the male bears to his own body, to that of the female, and to the child."

Henry Ward Beecher
(1813–1887)

"Marriage is the grave of love."

At the time that Henry Ward Beecher was accused of adultery, he was the most famous minister in America. His heartfelt sermons were a sharp break from the fire-and-brimstone, Old Testament–based rhetoric of the time. Beecher's signature "Gospel of Love" philosophy taught that Christ's love was unconditional—a cutting-edge theory in nineteenth-century America. Thousands of people flocked to hear him speak at the Plymouth Church every Sunday.

While his wife Eunice was giving birth to and raising their ten children, Beecher was busy as well. The charismatic preacher had been dogged by unproven rumors of sexual philandering throughout his career, including liaisons with poet Edna Dean Proctor and neighbor Chloe Beach, the latter reportedly giving birth to Beecher's illegitimate child. The affair that would prove to be his downfall, however, was with his parishioner Elizabeth Tilton.

Elizabeth was the wife of Beecher's good friend Theodore Tilton. Their dalliance allegedly began in October 1868 when Mrs. Tilton "surrendered" to Beecher's advances after a "long moral resistance." Beecher convinced her that their love was "pure" and that she remained "spotless and chaste" in God's eyes. This was, of course, "pure" bullshit: The Bible that Beecher read from every Sunday made no provisions for "purity of love" when it came to condemning adultery. Still, his sweet nothings worked on her . . . at least for a while. Mrs. Tilton confessed her sins to her husband in 1870. Although Theodore forgave Beecher, he was unable to keep the affair a secret.

Spouses aside, not everyone who learned of the affair was disappointed. Women's rights advocate Victoria Woodhull was a leader in the Free Love movement.* "Free Lovers" sought to liberate women from the "sexual slavery" of loveless marriages, and they were heavily criticized by religious leaders of the day—including by Beecher. To Woodhull's ears, Beecher's sex-capades sounded suspiciously like the actions of a closeted Free Lover—not those of a preacher upholding the integrity of the social institution of marriage. In fact, Woodhull had it on good authority that Beecher had once privately called marriage "the grave of love." Evidence of his affair was exactly the ammunition that the Free Lovers needed to take the moral high ground in the public debate over women's rights. Woodhull publicized

---

* One writer of the day, John B. Ellis, proclaimed that Free Lovers were "anxious to bring their vile principles into favor." Among the "vile principles": easy access to birth control, less regulation on divorce, and legal recourse against abusive husbands. According to Ellis, allowing such changes would "destroy the institution of marriage, . . . abolish the Christian religion, and . . . inaugurate a reign of lust."

Beecher's frolicking in a newspaper story in October 1872, hoping to expose the minister as a hypocrite. Bedlam ensued.

Mrs. Tilton retracted her side of the story, stating that she had not slept with the minister. (She separated from her husband, but *not* due to the adultery, she insisted.) Beecher was exonerated at an inquiry by the Plymouth Church; Mrs. Tilton was excommunicated from the same church.

Theodore Tilton, retracting his forgiveness, sued Beecher in civil court for engaging in "criminal conversation" with his wife (adultery was a crime in nineteenth-century America). The six-month trial enthralled the public, who unanimously declared it the greatest scandal of the 1800s. Beecher refused to lay his hand on the Bible or swear under oath before taking the stand. His contradictory and rambling testimony convinced his flock—and three of the twelve jurors—that he was guilty, but the trial ended in a hung jury. Eunice Beecher never left her husband's side, even when, three years later, Mrs. Tilton publicly admitted that she *had* in fact slept with Beecher.

The beleaguered minister fell out of favor with the public, due largely in part to the scandal, and died of a stroke on March 8, 1887. And despite all of the hand wringing, the institution of marriage and the Christian religion survived both the Free Love movement and the freely loving antics of Henry Ward Beecher.

IN HIS OWN WORDS
Beecher Did a Bad, Bad Thing

"In love, the freshness and charm of youth have caught men's attention, and they have pronounced the first love best; but it is the poorest. One does not know how to love till he has felt the discipline of life. Young love is a flame; very pretty, often very hot and fierce, but still only light and flickering. The love of the older and disciplined heart is as coals, deep-burning, unquench-able," Beecher wrote. Exactly how "disciplined" his adulterous heart was is questionable, but it definitely appears to have been "unquenchable."

John Calvin

(1509–1564)

"The veil of holy marriage allows husband and wife to give each other delight."

Perhaps no theologian has done more to shape our current Western views on love, marriage, and family than John Calvin. The influential French pastor helped to lead society out of the Dark Ages by redefining the roles of husbands and wives and introducing new divorce guidelines that allowed men and women alike to sue for custody and alimony.

Calvin was thirty years old by the time he began to seriously contemplate marriage for himself. Still at an early stage in his clerical career, he viewed wives as little more than glorified housekeepers. "I have never taken a wife," Calvin wrote, "and I do not know if I shall ever marry. If I did so, it would be to free myself from trivial worries so that I could devote myself to the Lord." His friends encouraged him to seek a companion. He laid out his ground rules for such a union, writing:

I am none of those insane lovers who embrace even vices, once they have been overcome by a fine figure. The only beauty that attracts me is this: if she is modest, accommodating, not haughty, frugal, patient, and there is hope she will be concerned about my health.

In early 1540, one of Calvin's supporters introduced him to a young German woman from a noble family. He was looking for a ~~housekeeper~~ wife whom he could converse with and foresaw communication problems with the German-speaking girl. He did not want to hurt her feelings; he grudgingly agreed to the wedding on the condition that she learn to speak French. Her family began planning a wedding for that spring. At the same time, Calvin dispatched his brother with the instructions to find a more suitable marriage candidate *quickly*. (His brother's search was ultimately a failure.) It is obvious that Calvin had little confidence that his fiancée would be able to learn French . . . and she apparently never did, as the wedding date came and went without any wedding bells.

Later that year, Calvin found a more agreeable marriage prospect in Idelette de Bure, a widowed member of his congregation. This new woman had experience running a household, and had two children from her previous marriage—practically a family starter kit in Calvin's eyes. Most importantly, she spoke his language. This time, Calvin went through with the nuptials.

Their first few weeks as a married couple were spent in bed . . . sick. Calvin believed that this was a warning from God not to enjoy the married life too fervently (although he had no moral qualms about others enjoying marriage—see "In His Own Words"). Despite the omen of their initial mutual illness, Calvin looked forward to having children of his own with Bure.

Sadly, their only child together did not survive infancy. Calvin was stoic about the tragedy, writing, "The Lord has given me a son, but he has also taken him away." Their marriage was otherwise uneventful. After Idelette passed away in 1549, Calvin did not remarry.

IN HIS OWN WORDS
Ain't No Shame

Unlike other biblical scholars of the Middle Ages, Calvin's views on sex were mostly positive. He believed that celibacy is not a part of God's plan: "It is tempting God to strive against the nature imparted by him, and to despise his present gifts as if they did not belong to us at all." Enjoying sex within marriage is a good thing. "Whatever sin or shame is in it," he wrote, "is so covered by the goodness of marriage that it ceases to be sin, or at least to be so regarded by God," for "the intercourse of husband and wife is a pure thing, good and holy." Amen.

Albert Camus

(1913–1960)

"Blessed are the hearts that can bend; they shall never be broken."

French Algerian Albert Camus is most closely associated with the philosophy of the absurd: Since death is inevitable, life is meaningless. Only this realization, he believed, can lead one to making the most of the here and now and living life to the fullest. Humanity should stop trying to impose order and meaning on an irrational universe. Such a position did not lend itself well to romance; nevertheless, Camus was not immune. As he wrote, "Love is the kind of illness that does not spare the intelligent or the dull."

He married his first wife, Simone Hié, in 1934. They were both young and Camus quickly came to believe that their union was a mistake, especially because Hié was a morphine addict and Camus was averse to drug use. Their marriage ended when Camus found out that his wife was having sex with a doctor in exchange for morphine. His divorce likely influenced the dark views on romantic love this line from his 1942 novel *The Stranger* suggests: "Attraction, marriage, and fidelity become synonyms for bondage."

Three months after his divorce was finalized, Camus married mathematician Francine Faure. Her sister thought that

Camus's ears protruded like a monkey's; Faure was in love and unfazed. "The monkey is the animal closest to man," she responded.

Both Faure and her "monkey" strayed. Unpublished letters revealed that she had a clandestine affair with the actress Maria Casares, while Camus pursued countless women behind his wife's back. In regard to Camus's extramarital affairs, biographer Olivier Todd said, "I did not write a book about Albert Camus's love life. Even a telephone directory wouldn't have been long enough for that!"

Camus remained wed to his second wife until he was killed in a car crash in 1960 at the age of forty-six.

IN HIS OWN WORDS
It's Not You, It's Me

Camus held his lovers at a distance. "All my life when someone has become attached to me, I've done everything to make them back off," he wrote in a letter. In another letter, he complained that he had "no gift for love." One of the characters in his novel *Caligula* voiced an opinion that could be construed as that of its author: "To love someone means to be willing to age with that person. I am not capable of such love."

Nicolas Chamfort
(1741–1794)

"The world either breaks or
hardens the heart."

When the principal at his Parisian school suggested that he become a priest, Sébastien Roch Nicolas quipped, "I'll never be a priest. I'm too fond of sleep, philosophy, women, honor and real fame."

In his late teens and early twenties, Nicolas blossomed as a playwright. He changed his name to "Nicolas Chamfort" to mask his peasant roots and shaved two years off his age to play up his role as a wunderkind. The studious and studly Chamfort rumpled the bedsheets of beautiful actresses and noblewomen, his stamina in the bedroom earning him the nickname "Hercules."* For a while, he lived out his fanciful dream of sleep, philosophy, women, honor, and fame.

Then, at the age of twenty-five, he lost everything.

An unknown (possibly venereal) disease struck Chamfort, leaving him unable to read, write, or even walk for several months. The mysterious ailment afflicted every part of his

---

* His greatest conquest was Mademoiselle Guimard, a forty-five-year-old dancer who, if a contemporary police report is to be believed, had the "finest breasts in the world."

body, from his nervous system to his digestive system. When he recovered from the illness, the playful, confident young man who had been the talk of the town was gone forever. A fire-breathing pessimist emerged from the ashes.

The reason for his change in attitude was readily apparent: The illness had permanently scarred his good looks and, more horrifically, disfigured his genitals, a devastating blow to a man who had previously placed such a high value on physical relationships. Chamfort was forced to contemplate how he had been living his life, and he did not like what he found: "The moment when youthful illusions and passions are shattered often provokes sorrow, but sometimes we come to hate the glamour which deceived us."

Love, to this point in his life, had been nothing more than "the contact of skins." The illness forced his heart into a state of exile, and fifteen years passed before he finally experienced the depths of true love with fifty-three-year-old widow Marthe Buffon.

"There existed something more and better than love [between us], since there was complete union on the level of ideas, feelings and attitudes," Chamfort later wrote about their romance. Unfortunately, his deformed member likely muted their sexual relationship. In 1782, Chamfort and Buffon moved to the country, where they found true happiness together. Chamfort loved Buffon "as ardently as a mistress, as tenderly as his mother," according to fellow writer Noël Aubin.

After just six months in the country, Buffon fell ill and died in her lover's arms. His happiness shattered again, Chamfort returned to Paris.

He made one last-ditch attempt at romance with Julie Careau, a twenty-two-year-old dancer. "Chamfort was smitten by a terrible fever of love that I had sparked in him, without the least intention of doing so," Julie wrote. Rejected, Chamfort gave up on love and resigned himself to his work for the final ten years of his life.

In 1793, faced with imprisonment over sarcastic remarks he had made against government officials, Chamfort attempted to commit suicide.* "Living is a disease from the pains of which sleep eases us every sixteen hours; sleep is but a palliative, death alone is the cure," he wrote.

IN HIS OWN WORDS
In 140 Characters or Less

Aphorisms are short, cynical witticisms drawn from personal experience. Nicolas Chamfort was the undisputed master of the

---

* His suicide was less than successful. Chamfort shot himself in the face—taking off his nose and part of his jaw—and stabbed himself in the neck and chest with a paper cutter. He was found unconscious in a pool of blood, the victim of twenty-two self-inflicted injuries. He lived another five months in excruciating pain before finally perishing from his infected wounds.

seventeenth- and eighteenth-century art form; here are some of his greatest hits:

- One must make the choice between loving women and knowing them; there is no middle course.
- Love resembles epidemic diseases: the more one fears them, the more liable is one to infection.
- Marriage follows on love as smoke on flame.
- Love gives greater pleasure than marriage for the same reason that romance [novels] are more amusing than history [books].

Auguste Comte
(1798–1857)

*"Gloomy and painful as celibacy is,
a bad marriage is much worse."*

When Auguste Comte left his house for an evening stroll on May 3, 1821, he did not expect to meet his future wife. The French philosopher's self-described "lack of charm and beauty" was of no help with the opposite sex, so he hoped only to pick up a lady of the night, strike up a temporary "business relationship," and head home to finish some writing. He met Caroline Massin, a prostitute of uncommon charm, and for the next six months "they saw each other whenever he could afford it," according to biographer Mary Pickering. Comte stopped visiting Massin after an old girlfriend popped back into his life in the fall of 1821.

A year later, he ran into Massin again. She had retired from her lucrative line of work and now ran a reading room. They struck up a more conventional friendship this time. Comte offered mathematics lessons to help her with bookkeeping for her new business; however, she had no inclination for legitimate work and sold her business after a short time, planning to move in with a wealthy businessman who had promised to support her. When the businessman changed his mind, she was faced with a return to life on the streets . . . unless, perhaps,

Comte would take her in. He consented, but admitted to being "a little tormented" over the decision: Although he was once again single, he could not see himself in a normal relationship with her and was adamant about keeping his hands off his new housemate.

As a former prostitute, Massin was required to undergo bi-weekly medical examinations. There was only one way to escape the exams and erase her name from the registry of working girls: marriage. Comte, angry at authorities and at the same time touched by her trust in him, agreed to marry her. They were wed on February 19, 1825, in the town hall.

After less than two tense years of marriage, Comte had a nervous breakdown that left him unable to write or teach. He spent his time alternately lying in bed and crouching behind doors like an animal. When his wife tried to intervene, Comte threw knives at her. His sanity came and went over the next year. Unable to pull himself together, he jumped off a bridge; a royal guard fished him out of the water. Comte made an "almost miraculous recovery," thanks to his wife's care—who, luckily for Comte, had not been frightened away by the flying knives.

Thirteen years later, their marriage was still on shaky ground. Comte and Massin were sleeping in separate bedrooms. "I have always thought that all that is lost between us should make what may remain more precious to us," Massin wrote to her husband in 1839, hinting at the possibility of a reunion. She wanted to rekindle their "very deep friendship," because he still occupied in her heart "a place that never could . . . be taken by anyone else."

However, Comte "wished only to be alone and tranquil." He believed that he would have completed his masterwork, *Cours*, in eight years—instead of twelve—without his wife in the picture. She seemed to agree, writing, "A man is not only in this world to write volumes on behalf of posterity [and] if there had been less science at home, there would have been far more happiness."

In all, there was so much science and so little happiness that they separated four times: in 1826, 1833, 1838, and 1842. After being berated by her husband for interrupting his work for the last time, she packed her bags for good. Divorce was illegal at the time, but Comte paid his wife three thousand francs a year so that he could live in peace. Perhaps their relationship had carried on far longer than it had any right to: She was a brash and opinionated former owner of two businesses and refused to bow to her husband. "My great crime was to see in you a husband, not a master. . . . Really, I did not know how to be submissive, but *even so*, I did love you," she wrote to her husband. She went on to be a governess while her husband continued his studies, unabated.

He pioneered the study of human social activity, coining the word "sociology" to describe his newly minted scientific field. But for all of the progress that Comte made in his work, he never successfully scrutinized the relationships in his own life. To the bitter end, he maintained that Caroline was the "sole irreparable mistake" in his life. "Unable to establish a truly loving relationship with his family or wife, Comte finally chose to find gratification in a love for humanity," Pickering wrote of Comte's ironic fate as an expert in social relations.

IN HIS OWN WORDS
Comte's Strange Gospel

For most intellectuals, founding a brand new scientific field would be legacy enough. Not for Comte, who also started his own religion. After splitting from his wife, he became obsessed with another woman, Clotilde de Vaux. Though they were not lovers, their intense friendship resulted in the foundations of a new secular religion: "Positivism," a scientifically based religious movement through which they intended to advance intellectual thought in a post-Enlightenment society. Comte rechristened his new friend "Saint Clotildes" in his manuscripts after she died in 1846.

The Positivism movement carried on without its patron saint. For his new religion, Comte copied Catholicism's most popular aspects. (Why mess with success?) Thus, the Holy Trinity was rebranded the "Positivist Trilogy" of the Great

Being, the Great Medium, and the Great Fetish. He even proposed a new calendar for his religion.* Comte had thought of everything, except for one key aspect: followers. Though his religion failed to catch on with more than a handful of hardcore devotees, it paved the way for the spread of secular humanist organizations in the nineteenth century.

---

* The months were renamed after historical and literary figure: Moses, Homer, Aristotle, Archimedes, Caesar, Saint Paul, Charlemagne, Dante, Gutenberg, Shakespeare, Descartes, Frederic, and Bichat. There were thirteen months instead of twelve. If Comte had kept the number of months at twelve (removing the obscure Bichat or Frederic, perhaps?), his calendar might have had a fighting chance.

René Descartes
(1596–1650)

"It is easy to hate and it is difficult to love."

October 15, 1634. The fateful night that French philosopher René Descartes—the man now known as the father of both modern philosophy and analytical geometry—lost his virginity to a serving maid, Hélène Jans. This single night of passion resulted in an illegitimate child.* Descartes never married Hélène, but he did gain custody of their daughter, Francine. He loved Francine very much and was excited about educating her. Unfortunately, she died of scarlet fever at the age of five.

Descartes, a devout Roman Catholic, repented of his fornication and dedicated himself to a celibate existence. "God quickly raised him above [his sin]," his biographer Adrien Baillet wrote.

He entered into the most emotionally intimate relationship of his life several years later with Princess Elizabeth, the twenty-five-year-old daughter of Frederick, King of Bohemia. Descartes was forty-seven when he and the princess first wrote

---

* This was, by all indications, the only time that Descartes ever engaged in sexual intercourse. To father a child on his first and only try meant that he was either extremely lucky or an excellent marksman.

to each other in 1643. After just a year of exchanging letters, Descartes dedicated his book *Principles of Philosophy* to her.

They met only a handful of times but corresponded extensively until Descartes's death in 1650. Elizabeth was his closest correspondent toward the end of his life, and it was "to some extent because of her great interest [in his intellectual endeavors] that he pursued the passions so assiduously," wrote biographer Stephen Gaukroger about Descartes's masterpiece *Passions*. Although the *Stanford Encyclopedia of Philosophy* asserts that the book was the "result of the probing of Princess Elizabeth," there was, alas, no probing going on between the two.*

IN HIS OWN WORDS
The Passion of Descartes

It is quite likely that Descartes believed Princess Elizabeth was his soulmate—if not in body, then at least in spirit. "Love is an

---

* The real problem with Princess Elizabeth may have been that she was *too* perfect. Descartes had a fetish for cross-eyed women: "When I was a child, I was in love with a girl of my own age who was slightly cross-eyed; consequently whenever I looked at her unfocused eyes the impression of that vision of her on my brain was so linked to what aroused the passion of love that, for long afterward, whenever I saw cross-eyed people I felt more inclined to love them than others."

emotion of the soul caused by a movement of the spirits, which impels the soul to join itself by will to objects that appear to be agreeable to it," Descartes wrote in one of the few actually passionate sections in *Passions*.

John Dewey
(1859–1952)

"Love's garden is a stony place with weeds."

When American educational theorist John Dewey was a college student at Johns Hopkins University, he was so painfully shy that university president Daniel Coit Gilman actually advised him not to be so bookish. "Don't live such a secluded life; get out and see people," Gilman told Dewey.

It turns out that Dewey just needed to find the right girl. Shortly after meeting Alice Chipman in a university class, he began talking about marriage. "There was a full-sized moral and intellectual admiration between them," wrote Dewey's student Max Eastman. "No two people were ever more in love," Dewey once told Eastman. In July 1886, after Alice graduated from college and Dewey was promoted to assistant professor, they married.

The "moral and intellectual admiration" was not enough to keep Dewey entirely faithful over the next four decades of their marriage. Anzia Yezierska, a Polish American writer who was twenty years Dewey's junior, sat in on his lectures at Columbia College. The good professor had a short-lived but emotional affair with her in 1918. "Physically, the relationship appears not to have advanced beyond light petting," biographer Robert B. Westbrook wrote.

Dewey's wife Alice passed away in 1927. Nearly two decades later, when he was eighty-seven, Dewey married Roberta Grant, a forty-two-year-old widow. They did not announce their marriage because Dewey feared that she would face criticism due to the difference in their ages. Still, Dewey's second marriage caused rifts between him and his children. Evelyn, Dewey's daughter from his first marriage, warned her father's friends that Roberta was pouring "evil fantasies" into Dewey's head. Roberta was a "paranoiac" and a "liar," according to biographer Sidney Hook. Estranged from his family and friends, Dewey passed away quietly at the age of ninety-two.

IN HIS OWN WORDS
Not-So-Great Love Letters of Great Men

Despite his considerable verbal prowess in other areas, Dewey's love letters to Alice "are so extraordinarily unsophisticated that the reader can only suppose the writer of these . . . lacked practice in opening his heart to anyone," wrote biographer Alan Ryan. Is he being too harsh on the man? Read the following excerpts from Dewey's letters yourself and be the judge:

> Sweetest when are you coming back to bless me with
> the beloved joy beyond joy of your love? Loved one of
> my soul, myself, my own true self, my awakener of life

and desire, my fullness of life and satisfaction of want, my source of all that I can be, and giver of all that I am—do I say that I love you? . . . Oh, my lover darling, it is the thought that I can give you love which thrills me through and through with the joy of life. . . .

My love, how your love fills everything. Darling, it is me and everything about me. I am it and I am in it, my own love, and it is the sweetness of the world. Darling, how can I but love you with my life, with my being, with my all, which yet is not mine, but yours sweet one.

Denis Diderot
(1713–1784)

"It has been said that love robs those who have it of their wit, and gives it to those who have none."

When Denis Diderot decided to become a writer at the age of twenty-one, he had already attempted and failed at careers as a clergyman, a doctor, and a lawyer. While these other occupations paid more, Diderot's heart was set on the literary life. For the next ten years, he lived hand-to-mouth, making money doing translations, writing sermons, and tutoring students.* The bohemian existence "has been often made to sound romantic on paper . . . [yet] it was squalid and shabby enough in reality," author Evelyn Beatrice Hall wrote of Diderot's struggles to make it as a freelance writer in eighteenth-century France.

In 1743, Diderot was lodging with a poor seamstress and her mother. The seamstress, Antoinette Champion, was uneducated, but she captured the philosopher's heart nonetheless. To spark a relationship, he asked Antoinette to sew him an outfit, claiming that he would be entering the Jesuit seminary and

---

* The tutoring was short-lived. "I am making men of your children, perhaps; but they are fast making a child of me," a frustrated Diderot told the father of one of his pupils.

was in dire need of clothing. (He had no such plans.) Luckily for him, Diderot's skillful banter was more charming than the elaborate ruse would suggest. They soon married.

Diderot's jealousy quickly got the better of him. He asked his new wife to stop sewing, afraid that her business would bring her into contact with other desperate bachelors looking for love. With only Diderot's sporadic sources of income and Antoinette's mother's meager savings, the threesome continued to live in poverty. "The ever popular Diderot was often asked out to dine with his friends, and always went; while at home [his wife and mother-in-law] feasted on dry bread," Hall wrote.

In addition to the inevitable fights over money that ensued, Diderot found the realities of married life constrictive to his bohemian sensibilities. He decided that passions could not be contained by "a senseless vow" like marriage. "What a noble aim is that of the zealot who tortures himself like a madman in order to desire nothing [and] love nothing," he wrote. Lovers are passions to be pursued, not held captive. While Antoinette was away visiting family, Diderot began an affair with Madame de Puisieux.

Madame was a clothes hound. She drained Diderot of what money he did have but, ironically, provided the muse for some of his best-known works: "Essay on Merit and Virtue" and "Philosophical Thoughts." One day, she showed up to visit Diderot dressed in extravagant clothes that he had not bought for her. Diderot followed her and caught her with another man. The jealous philosopher "renounced her as easily and hotly as he had fallen in love with her," according to Hall.

His next infatuation was with Sophie Volland. They traded letters for twenty-eight years, many of which were later burned by Diderot's wife. Scholars have speculated that Diderot and Volland were lovers, but any concrete evidence of such an affair likely went up in flames.

Diderot's writing eventually made him famous, and he became a wealthy man when he sold his personal library of books to Catherine the Great. His wife gave birth to a daughter, but their troubled marriage never improved; his depression following Sophie Volland's sudden death in 1784 did not help matters.

Nine months after Volland passed away, Diderot died suddenly while eating an apricot at the dinner table with his family. His last words were: "What possible harm could it do to me?"

IN HIS OWN WORD
Burn After Reading

Many of Diderot's love letters to Sophie Volland were (unsurprisingly) burned by his wife, but some survived:

July 1759: I am wholly yours—you are everything to me; we will sustain each other in all the ills of life it may please fate to inflict upon us; you will soothe my troubles; I will comfort you in yours. . . . Is it not true, my dear Sophie, that you are very amiable? Examine yourself—see how worthy you are of being loved; and know that I love you very much. . . . I am as happy as man can be in knowing that I am loved by the best of women.

October 20, 1759: You love me. You will always love me. I believe you: now I am happy. I live again. I can talk, work, play, walk—do anything you wish. . . . I would love you even more than I do, if I knew how.

Diogenes the Cynic
(c. 412–323 BC)

"Marriage is never any good to a man,
and we must be quite content
if it does no harm."

Diogenes the Cynic fought a lifelong battle against customs and traditions in the Greek world. His philosophy held that what is natural cannot be wrong. He took this as an excuse to fart, urinate, defecate, and masturbate in public.*

Nevertheless, Diogenes was an entertaining character and well liked by his fellow Athenians. Alexander the Great is said to have been a fan of the eccentric philosopher, remarking, "If I were not Alexander, I should wish to be Diogenes."

The historical record is ambiguous as to whether Diogenes ever fell in love; it's likely he never did, especially in light of his flagrant behavior. He did not believe that a truly wise man could ever be in love. Love, Diogenes said, is the province of men with nothing to do—an ironic sentiment coming from a man who slept outdoors in a barrel and begged for change during the day.

---

* When questioned about masturbating in public, Diogenes said, "I only wish I could be rid of hunger by rubbing my belly."

IN HIS OWN WORDS
The Perfect Gift

Diogenes abhorred social conventions such as marriage. "Humans have complicated every simple gift of the gods," he said, reasoning that marriage needlessly complicated the natural gift of sex. He proposed an alternative society in which women would be "possessed in common" by men. Instead of being paired off in monogamous marriages, men and women would be able to change sex partners as often as they liked in Diogenes's perfect world.

Fyodor Dostoyevsky
(1821–1881)

*"Love in action is a harsh and dreadful thing
compared with love in dreams."*

Russian author Fyodor Dostoyevsky, whose work influenced twentieth-century existentialists such as Albert Camus and Jean-Paul Sartre (pages 45 and 138), met Maria Dmitrievna Isayeva while serving as a private in the Siberian Regiment in 1856. Their chances of hooking up were improbable: She was already married and, in contrast to the gloomy Dostoyevsky, was both attractive and vivacious. "I do not think that she highly esteemed him," their mutual friend Baron Alexander Vrangel wrote. "It was more that she pitied him. . . . In love with him she most decidedly never was." Maria saw Dostoyevsky as a poor man "without a future." Still, she apparently pitied him enough to marry him in 1857 after her first husband passed away.

Their relationship was a rocky one. "We were both thoroughly unhappy, but could not cease from loving one another; the more wretched we were, the more we clung together," Dostoyevsky later wrote in a letter to Vrangel. "In fact the more unhappy we became, the closer our bond became. No matter how strange that may seem, it was so."

When Dostoyevsky was diagnosed with epilepsy, he received a medical discharge from the army and returned with his bride to his hometown of St. Petersburg. The move turned out to be fatal to Maria. She had tuberculosis, and the damp climate in the new city exacerbated her condition.

While her health deteriorated, the forty-year-old Dostoyevsky began a romantic relationship with twenty-two-year-old writer Apollinaria Suslova in 1862. She remained his mistress for the next couple of years, but the situation was mutually unsatisfactory. They broke off relations in 1864. The thinly veiled autobiographical narrator of Dostoyevsky's novel *The Gambler*, written near the end of his affair with Suslova, has this to say:

> There were moments (every time we ended a conversation, as a matter of fact) when I would have given up half my life to strangle her. I swear that had I the chance to thrust a sharp knife slowly into her bosom I believe I would have done it with delight.

Following his breakup with Suslova, Dostoyevsky spent more time attending to his sick wife. While he was writing *Notes from Underground*, he listened to his wife's hacking cough in the next room. "Every day there is a moment when we expect her to die," he wrote. She finally did so on April 15, 1864, and his journal entry from the next day is heartbreaking in its brevity: "April 16. Masha [Maria] is lying on the table. Will I ever see Masha again?"

His wife's death began a dark time in Dostoyevsky's life. His brother passed away shortly thereafter. Dostoyevsky's gambling addiction worsened, and his debts mounted exponentially. A halfhearted proposal to his former mistress Suslova was rejected. Redemption would come for him in the form of a twenty-year-old stenographer, Anna Grigorievna Snitkina.

In October 1866, Dostoyevsky hired Snitkina to transcribe his work. It was not love at first sight: "Nothing can convey the pitiful appearance of Fyodor . . . when I met him for the first time. He seemed confused, anxious, helpless, lonely, irritable, and almost ill," she wrote of the forty-six-year-old author.

As he dictated his writing to her, an attraction grew in both of their hearts. After working together for less than a month, he tossed out an idea to her for a new novel about an elderly artist who falls in love with a young woman . . . named Anna. Would it be possible for such a relationship to work, he asked? It would, she responded, because true love is not confined to appearances. Growing more confident that his gambit would succeed, he ventured further. "Put yourself in her place. Imagine that this artist, that is I, confessed that he loved you and asked you to be his wife. What would you say?"

She did not hesitate in her response: "I would answer that I love you and will love you all my life." They were married three months later.

The early years of their marriage were tainted by Dostoyevsky's gambling problems. He rewarded his new wife's tolerant attitude toward his behavior by pawning her jewelry and wedding ring. (Anna eventually recovered the ring.) After his children were born, Dostoyevsky's gambling slowed. And although they continued to experience financial difficulties, Dostoyevsky and Anna enjoyed a tranquil family life until he passed away in 1881.

IN HIS OWN WORDS
Live and Let Die

There was no point in holding a grudge following a failed relationship, Dostoyevsky reasoned. The changing tides of romance did not bother him: "We should be eternally grateful to a woman whom we have loved, for every day and hour of joy which she has given us. We may not demand from her that she think of us only all her life long."

Friedrich Engels
(1820–1895)

*"Examples of faithful monogamy among birds
do not furnish any proofs for men,
for we are not descended from birds."*

German socialist Friedrich Engels did not believe that monogamy was the natural state of man. He dismissed anecdotal evidence in animals as irrelevant to the argument. He wrote:

> If strict monogamy is the height of virtue, then the palm belongs to the tapeworm that carries a complete male and female sexual apparatus in each of its 50 to 200 sections and passes its whole lifetime in fertilizing itself in every one of its sections.

Engels lived by his words, rarely tying himself down to one woman throughout his lifetime. In an 1846 letter, Friedrich Engels tried to persuade his good friend Karl Marx to visit him in Paris.

> If I had an income of 5000 francs I would do nothing but work and amuse myself with women until I went to pieces. If there were no Frenchwomen, life wouldn't be worth living. But so long as there are *grisettes*, well and good!

Grisettes were working-class French women. They worked in the garment industry by day and flirted with men by night. They were not prostitutes (at least not all of them), but they had an infamous reputation for being "easy."* Still, Engels condemned prostitution as "the most tangible exploitation—one directly attacking the physical body—of the proletariat by the bourgeoisie."

Engels enjoyed many female companions, from the aforementioned *grisettes* in Paris to a pair of illiterate Irish sisters whom he dated in succession. He even married one of the sisters, Lizzy Burns, despite his intense dislike of marriage. It turns out that the civil ceremony was an entirely charitable gambit on Engels's part, as he wed Lizzy on her deathbed.

When Karl Marx fathered a child with his housekeeper, Helene Demuth, Engels stepped in to protect his married friend's reputation. When paternity rumors began circulating, Engels deflected suspicion from Marx by hinting that it was his, and not Marx's, son. This explanation sufficed for Marx's wife, apparently, since Demuth never lost her job as a housekeeper in the Marx household. The boy's father's identity was kept secret until Engels's deathbed confession.

---

* Mark Twain didn't care how easy they were. He wrote that *grisettes* were "like nearly all the Frenchwomen I ever saw—homely."

IN HIS OWN WORDS
The Swinger's Manifesto

The nuclear family—husband, wife, and children—was a bourgeois product of capitalism. According to Marx and Engels's *Communist Manifesto*, this traditional family structure was founded "on capital, on private gain." They went a step further, damning all marriages as restrictive. "All that this Protestant monogamy achieves is a conjugal partnership of leaden boredom, known as 'domestic bliss.'"

Engels believed that things would change once the communist revolution came to fruition. "True equality between men and women can become a reality only when the exploitation of both by capital has been abolished," Engels wrote. Without private property, traditional families would disintegrate and the wife swapping could commence.

Johann Wolfgang von Goethe
(1749–1832)

*"Love is an ideal thing, marriage is a real thing;
a confusion of the real with the ideal
never goes unpunished."*

Johann Wolfgang von Goethe was one of the first German romantics to turn suffering into an art form. He developed a series of crushes on unattainable women over the course of his life, resulting in a perpetually broken heart that fueled his writing.

He first fell in love at the tender age of fifteen with one of his schoolmates. "She gave her hand to no one, not even to me; she allowed no touch; yet she many times seated herself near me," Goethe wrote optimistically of the unnamed girl. "If, however, I ventured . . . toward her, she withdrew."* At one point, he succeeded in getting a kiss from the young woman, planted squarely on his forehead. "It was the first and last time that she granted me this favor; for, alas, I was not to see her again."

She left town; Goethe was later crushed to hear that she had referred to him as a child. "Her cold and repelling manner, which had before so charmed me, now seemed to me quite repugnant," he wrote. "This arrow with its barbed hooks was torn out of my heart."

---

* She may have read some of the erotic poetry that he wrote in his spare time. Here's a taste from one of his later poems, "Elf King": "I love you, your fair form excites me; and if you are not willing I shall use force."

Young Goethe became depressed. He did not eat or sleep well. The effects of the affair remained with Goethe throughout his life; he refers to it as his great "misfortune" in his autobiography, lamenting that she had been "taken away" from him (when, clearly, he had never possessed her in the first place).

As an adult, he fell madly in love with his friend Charlotte von Stein. There are no indications that she reciprocated his feelings—she was married and had seven children competing for her attention. Yet Goethe made no attempts to conceal his infatuation with her and made overtures toward her for the twelve years that he lived near her family. She accepted his friendship but politely deflected his come-ons. Goethe eventually left for Italy, and they corresponded until her death in 1827.

True sexual relationships appear to have been stunted by Goethe's "secret" love for his younger sister Cornelia. Goethe had a hard time keeping secrets, however, and wrote about their taboo love in his autobiography. "[She assured] me that I was the only one who truly loved, understood, and esteemed her. . . . We both thought ourselves infinitely unhappy, and the more so as, in this singular case, the confidants could not change themselves into lovers."

Cornelia's marriage shattered his fantasies, but it may have also prompted Goethe to step up his game. He met Christiane Vulpius, the first woman to truly return his feelings. He lost his virginity to her, narrowly avoiding the stigma of being labeled a forty-year-old virgin by less than a year. They lived together as common-law man and wife and had several children together, eventually marrying in 1806.

After Christiane's death in 1816, he fell in love with another young woman, Ulrike von Levetzow. Ulrike's mother disliked him; he never worked up the courage to propose to Ulrike. For Goethe, the unattainable was far more romantic anyway.

IN HIS OWN WORDS
The Suicide King

Unrequited love affairs were the plague of Johann Wolfgang von Goethe's existence until he was nearly forty. These affairs—all unconsummated—provided the raw material for his poetry and prose.

The book that shot Goethe into the stratosphere of literary superstardom, *The Sorrows of Young Werther*, was an epistolary novel about a man who falls in love with a married woman. Young Werther's love is not returned in kind. "Sometimes I tell myself my fate is unique," Werther says in the novel. "Consider all other men fortunate, I tell myself; no one has ever suffered like you."

Spoiler alert! Young Werther, tired of living in a state of agony, shoots himself at the end of the novel. Goethe based the character of Werther on his friend Jerusalem who had killed himself in the same manner following a love affair. Goethe had often grappled with suicidal thoughts himself:

> Among a considerable collection of weapons, I possessed a handsome, well polished dagger. This I laid every night by my bed, and before I extinguished the candle, I tried whether I could succeed in plunging the sharp point a couple of inches deep into my heart.

He credits the act of writing *Werther* for lifting his own symptoms of depression. The novel was to have the opposite effect on the public.

The book was a literary sensation across Europe upon its publication in 1774. Scores of young, heartbroken men dressed in yellow trousers, blue jackets, and open-necked shirts in emulation of Goethe's protagonist. Unfortunately, many young men also paid tribute to their new hero by committing suicide.

Copycat suicides racked up across the continent. "For as it requires but a little match to blow up an immense mine, so the explosion which followed my publication was mighty," Goethe wrote. Authorities in Italy, Germany, and Denmark banned the book in an attempt to keep it from completely infecting a generation of disaffected youth. Eventually, the subculture of suffering that the book had spawned fell out of fashion, just like any other fad.*

---

* Only to be revived (minus the suicides) by the English rock group The Cure in the early 1980s.

Georg Wilhelm Friedrich Hegel
(1770–1831)

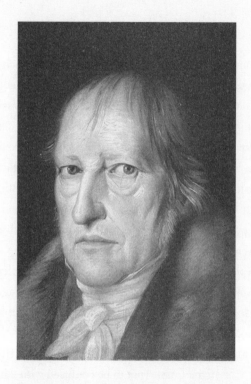

*"The difference between man and woman
is the same as between animal and plant."*

German philosopher Georg Wilhelm Friedrich Hegel wrote, "Love can only take place towards an equal, the mirror, the echo of our own being." Since humanity was created in God's image, he reasoned, God is the only equal deserving of true love; earthly romance is but a shallow approximation of divine love. This did not prevent Hegel from fathering an illegitimate son with his landlord's wife, Christiana Burkhardt. Although Christiana was separated from her husband, Hegel feared reprisal from his landlord and left town a month after his child was born.

In September 1811, the forty-year-old Hegel married Maria Helena Susanna von Tucher, a svelte woman half his age. They had two sons of their own and even accepted his illegitimate son by Christiana into their family in 1816.

The marriage created a devastating rift between Hegel and his sister Christiane Luane (not to be confused with Christiana Burkhardt, the mother of his first son). Hegel invited Christiane into his family's home to assist with household chores while his wife was pregnant with their first child. Hegel confided in his sister that his goal in marriage was not happiness but "being contented." Christiane, who had always been close to her brother, flew into a rage and left the household, prompting speculation that she had become unnaturally attached to him and could not bear to see him with a woman whom he admittedly did not love.

Hegel feared that his sister was mentally ill and distanced himself and his new family from her. In 1831, three months after Hegel passed away, Christiane confirmed those suspicions when she drowned herself.

IN HIS OWN WORDS
This One's for the Ladies

Hegel's misogynistic beliefs were an anachronism even in the early nineteenth century, when his contemporary Arthur Schopenhauer (page 143) called him "a lasting monument to German stupidity." Hegel's views have not aged well, as you can see from this brief snippet:

> Women can, of course, be educated, but their minds are not adapted to the higher sciences, philosophy, or certain of the arts. Women may have happy inspirations, taste, elegance, but they have not the ideal. The difference between man and woman is the same as between

animal and plant. The animal corresponds more closely to the character of the man, the plant to that of the woman. . . . If woman were to control the government, the state would be in danger, for they do not act according to the dictates of universality, but are influenced by accidental inclinations and opinions.

Martin Heidegger
(1889–1976)

*"Why is love rich beyond all other possible
human experiences and a sweet burden to
those seized in its grasp?"*

German professor Martin Heidegger's work is not recommended for the beginning student of philosophy. His books are filled with maxims such as " 'Being' is not something like a being. . . . What determines beings as beings, that in terms of which beings are already understood." Thankfully, an advanced degree is not required to understand his love life.

Heidegger married Elfriede Petri in 1917. They remained together for nearly sixty years, never separating or divorcing despite Heidegger's widely documented extramarital activities with his students.

Of Heidegger's trysts, his relationship with student Hannah Arendt was the most significant. "Dear Miss Arendt! I must see you this evening and speak to your heart," he wrote to his eighteen-year-old pupil. When she visited his University of Marburg office that night, the two made love for the first time. That they were student and teacher was merely an inconvenience, an "occasion" that "happened" to them. "I will never be able to call you mine, but from now on you will belong in my life," Heidegger wrote to his apt pupil. For the next four years, they would carry on a passionate physical affair, meeting in his office and the woods near the university campus. When Heidegger joined the Nazi Party in 1933, the Jewish Arendt fled to America.

Postwar, Arendt sought to resume her friendship (but not the affair) with Heidegger. Arendt was now married but still believed that she, and not Elfriede, had been the love of Heidegger's life. After Arendt met with Heidegger in 1950, she publicly defended him from criticism of his Nazi past. Professor Elzbieta Ettinger, author of *Hannah Arendt/Martin Heidegger*, told the *New York Times* that "no person who knows about love and passion will consider Arendt's forgiveness of Heidegger unusual. . . . Love is irrational. There is nothing we can do about it."

Heidegger's wife's own extramarital activities were eventually revealed: It turns out that their son Hermann was actually the fruit of an affair between Mrs. Heidegger and a family friend, a secret only brought to light with the 2005 publication of *Letters to His Wife: 1915–1970*, a collection of Heidegger's correspondence with his wife.

IN HIS OWN WORDS
The Heidegger Code

Even on a topic such as love, Heidegger's writing was more obfuscating than enlightening. Novice cryptographers are invited to take a crack at deciphering his words:

We change ourselves into that which we love, and yet remain ourselves. Then we would like to thank the beloved, but find nothing that would do it adequately. We can only be thankful to ourselves. Love transforms gratitude into faithfulness to ourselves and into an unconditional faith in the Other. Thus love steadily expands its most intimate secret. Closeness here is existence in the greatest distance from the other—the distance that allows nothing to dissolve—but rather presents the "thou" in the transparent, but "incomprehensible" revelation of the "just there." That the presence of the other breaks into our own life—this is what no feeling can fully encompass.

David Hume
(1711–1776)

"I had my choice of the person with whom I would conjoin myself in marriage. I had my choice, it is true, of my prison; but this is but a small comfort, since it must still be a prison."

According to his colleague Denis Diderot (page 67), David Hume resembled "a well-fed Bernardine monk." The *Stanford Encyclopedia of Philosophy* is much kinder to the Scottish economist, calling Hume "the most important philosopher ever to write in English."

Hume believed that romantic love "is derived from the conjunction of three different impressions or passions":

1. The pleasing sensation arising from beauty
2. The bodily appetite to reproduce
3. A generous kindness or goodwill

There is no indication that any of these passions ever resulted in love for Hume himself. The closest thing to a romantic relationship in his life was his friendship with the French socialite Comtesse de Boufflers. They corresponded before meeting in France in 1763. Although they spent much time together over the next year, they never became sexually involved. She eventually dropped him in order to pursue her more appealing lover, the Prince de Conti.

The comtesse's cold shoulder barely fazed Hume. "As I took a particular pleasure in the company of modest women, I had no reason to be displeased with the reception I met with from them," he wrote matter-of-factly.

IN HIS OWN WORDS
The Blame Game

Hume wrote that women want dominion over men and men want dominion over women. He found both sexes at fault in this eternal power struggle, but it was man who started it: "If we did not abuse our authority [over women], they would never think it worthwhile to dispute it."

Immanuel Kant
(1724–1804)

"Sexual union is the reciprocal use that one human being makes of the sexual organs and capacities of another."

German philosopher Immanuel Kant was "drier than dust, both in body and mind," according to contemporary Johann Friedrich Reichardt. Kant lived every day according to a set schedule, and neighbors set their clocks by his evening walks. He never even perspired—not once in his life. It should come as no surprise then that his love life was equally dry.

Kant believed that premarital sex—and any sexual act engaged in for ends other than procreation—is immoral. Additionally, sexual desire in itself is wrong since it turns a person "into an object. . . . As soon as the person is possessed, and the appetite sated, they are thrown away, as one throws away a lemon after squeezing the juice from it."

Sexual desire is only permissible in marriage when both parties turn each other into equal objects of desire. He equated premarital sex to sexual slavery, since one's sexuality is given without a contract guaranteeing equality between both parties. "It is not only admissible for the sexes to surrender and to accept each other for enjoyment under the condition of marriage, but it is possible for them to do so only under this condition." Kant viewed marriage as a contract for copulation whereby both parties gain "lifelong possession of each other's sexual attributes."

It is unsurprising that he never found a woman who agreed with his clinical view of marriage. Over the years, two women interested him, but Kant never pursued either of them. "When I needed a wife, I could not support one," he later lamented, citing his poverty as the primary reason he never attempted to tie the knot. In truth, it is inconceivable that Kant would have tolerated any disruption to his highly regimented daily schedule.

IN HIS OWN WORDS
Hand Check!

Although Kant had little to no experience with women, it appears that he had even less experience with himself. He refused to even name the "ultimate sin" of self-stimulation, but we can easily read between the lines:

> That such an unnatural use (and so misuse) of one's sexual attribute is a violation of duty to oneself, and indeed contrary to morality in its highest degree, occurs to everyone immediately, with the thought of it, and stirs up an aversion to this thought to such an extent that it is considered indecent even to call this vice by its proper

name. . . . In the case of unnatural vice it is as if man in general felt ashamed of being capable of treating his own person in such a way, which debases him beneath the beasts.

Kant believed that masturbation is a sin worse than "even murdering oneself." Suicide, he argued, requires courage; the masturbator is simply giving in weakly to lust.

Søren Kierkegaard
(1813–1855)

"Love is all, it gives all, and it takes all."

Søren Kierkegaard, the Danish father of existentialism, first felt the sting of love when he was twenty-four years old.* Regine Olsen, then only fifteen years old, caught the moody philosopher's eye. The infatuation temporarily interrupted his perpetual state of melancholy. "My God, why should these feelings awaken just now—oh, how alone I feel!" Kierkegaard wrote in his diary regarding his love for the young girl.

A true gentleman, Kierkegaard waited until she was eighteen to propose to her. "I have wanted you for two years," he told her after she was of age. She was silent at first, then mentioned that she was seeing one of her former teachers. Kierkegaard didn't care. "I have first priority," he said with authority. She was silent again. He finally left without an answer.

---

* Or did he feel the "sting of love" earlier? There's an oft-repeated story that Kierkegaard visited a brothel a year before meeting Regine Olsen and was forever shamed by the memory. A journal entry from 1836 mentioned a vague incident with "bestial giggling" that could be interpreted as a veiled reference to such a visit. "As an episode in his rowdy, hard-drinking student life at the time, it seems not unlikely," John Updike wrote.

Kierkegaard, not to be discouraged, paid a visit to Regine's father. Her dad "said neither yes nor no," but granted the young lover another meeting with his daughter. When Kierkegaard made his second proposal attempt, Regine succumbed to his persistence and accepted.

Far from being elated, Kierkegaard's depression worsened.

He hid his dark thoughts from his new fiancée—so successfully that, after a year of engagement, he confidently said that "she really did not know me." Rather than infect Regine with his despair, he sought to end the engagement with as little fanfare as possible by breaking up with her via letter. She wrote back that he could do "anything with her, absolutely anything" . . . except leave her.

For the next two months, he acted caddish toward Regine, playing the part of a villain in hopes that his beloved would leave him. Kierkegaard reflected that the time was "fearfully painful—having to be so cruel, and loving her as I did."

When their engagement ultimately ended after thirteen months, Olsen asked Kierkegaard if he would ever get married. "Yes, in ten years time . . . I will need a lusty girl to rejuvenate me," he told her in an attempt to drive her away from him forever. She asked him to kiss her, and he did: "But without passion—Merciful God!" he remarked. Regine went on to marry John Frederik (Fritz) Schlegel, the former teacher she had been seeing before Kierkegaard's proposal.

Kierkegaard was forever troubled by his betrayal of Regine.

He worried that "she would go out of her mind if she found out how things really were." For the next decade and a half, Kierkegaard buried himself in his religious writings. (He never did marry a "lusty girl.") In his will, Kierkegaard left everything that he owned to Regine, since he believed that their engagement was still "as binding as a marriage." Her husband had a very different interpretation and declined the inheritance on Regine's behalf.

IN HIS OWN WORDS
Always on His Mind

To devote oneself to another person completely, the lover must drop his or her defenses. This leaves lovers in a vulnerable position. Kierkegaard believed that lovers are never truly alone in their quests since God is always looking out for them:

> The one who in love forgets himself, forgets his suffering, in order to think of someone else's, forgets all his misery in order to think of someone else's, forgets what he himself loses in order lovingly to bear in mind someone else's loss, forgets his own advantage in order lovingly to think of someone else's—truly, such a person is not forgotten. There is one who is thinking about him: God in heaven.

John Locke
(1632–1704)

"There is no necessity in the nature of marriage, nor to the ends of it, that it should always be for life."

Thomas Jefferson once wrote that English philosopher John Locke was one of the "three greatest men that have ever lived, without any exception." As a political theorist, Locke laid the philosophical foundations for the United States Constitution with his writings on individual freedom and property rights. Yet in his pursuit of the political, Locke sacrificed the personal: He never married or had any children of his own.

The charming Locke certainly befriended many women over the years. It is apparent that at least some of them wanted to be more than just his pen pals, something that Locke was too aloof to recognize. The language he used toward his friend Elinor Parry, for instance, was tinged with the glow of romance in the beginning. He described her as "robbing me of the use of my reason," adding that "love is a fire and a flame full of heat and warmth." They exchanged flirtatious letters for a couple of years, but he never took any definitive steps toward courting her—even though Parry hinted on several occasions that Locke was free to reveal his passions. When subtlety proved useless, she boldly asked if he was now indifferent "of the affection you have framed in my soul?" Immediately, Locke's letters lost their flirtatiousness. In her final letter, Parry wrote:

> How hard is it for you to disguise your thoughts, soul and heart to one that knows it so well as I do. . . . You love me still. . . . [We will meet,] I believe, in the next world, since we will not in this.*

Locke's longest friendship was with Damaris Cudworth. They first began corresponding with each other in 1682 when she was twenty-three and he was forty-nine years old. After Cudworth became engaged to Sir Francis Masham, she wrote to Locke that a mutual friend told her "that you love me exceedingly." She was "really vexed" by this, and clearly hoped to draw out Locke's true feelings for her.

Locke, who was in Holland at the time, did not ride in on horseback and carry her away. Instead, he penned a letter, which she received on the day of her wedding. While she didn't save it, the letter was not the declaration of true love that Cudworth had been hoping for, and so she walked down the aisle and into her new role as a wife and mother.

Later, the newly christened Lady Masham emphasized that the intellectual bond that she shared with Locke would not be destroyed by her marriage: "The objects of all my thoughts are

---

* Locke is no doubt still trying to fend off her advances in the afterlife.

of an immortal nature; and such without doubt is friendship."
While Locke was still in Holland, Lady Masham gave birth to
her only child.

Locke returned to England in 1691 and Lady Masham
invited him to live in her home. It can safely be assumed
that there was no hanky-panky going on, as Locke was in
poor health during the final years of his life. In a letter to a
friend, Locke wrote, "I do not find that my age hath much inclined me to the thoughts of [love]. My health . . . is the only
mistress."

Locke lived with the Mashams until his death in 1704. He
left his estate to Masham's son, Francis Cudworth Masham. The
epitaph on Locke's gravestone reads in part, "His virtues, if indeed he had any, were too slight to be lauded by him or to be an
example to you. Let his vices be buried with him."

IN HIS OWN WORDS
My Baby Don't Mess Around

John Locke believed that a man in love exemplifies humankind's
capacity for self-deception.

Sometimes the force of a clear argument may make
some impression, yet they nevertheless stand firm, and

keep out the enemy, truth, that would captivate or disturb them. Tell a man passionately in love, that he is
jilted; bring a score of witnesses of the falsehood of his
mistress, it is 10 to one but three kinds of words of hers
shall invalidate all their testimonies.

Titus Lucretius
(c. 99–c. 55 BC)

*"It's easier to avoid the snares of love
than to escape once you are in that net."*

Roman philosopher Titus Lucretius's only surviving work is the philosophical poem *On the Nature of Things*, and little is known about Lucretius's life except for gossip and speculation. The most persistent legend involves a woman scorned, poison, hallucinations, and suicide—all key ingredients for a ripping yarn.

"Women are meretricious schemers who lay snares," Lucretius wrote. His opinion was supposedly based upon personal experience, related in the legend of the love potion (first transcribed by Jerome in the fourth century).

Lucretius's wife Lucilla, tired of being ignored as her husband worked on his poetry, employed a witch to brew a love potion. However, things did not go quite as planned. When Lucretius ingested the potion, he experienced horrifying visions of "the Epicurean universe with atoms colliding randomly in the void," according to author Lord Tennyson. Instead of falling deeply in love with his wife, Lucretius fell in love with "the highest Epicurean virtue of tranquility."

Lucretius addressed the divine tranquility directly in a series of books written "during the intervals of his insanity," but, never receiving a response from the universe, committed suicide at the age of forty-four by driving a knife into his own side.

IN HIS OWN WORDS
Now I Ain't Saying She a Gold Digger

Sex was morally acceptable for Lucretius, only so long as love was not involved. The man who finds himself in love is simply walking wounded, a slave to his lover's passions.

> *They pine away with wounds that none can see.*
> *Remember too their strength still wastes away,*
> *Their labor naught avails: their life is lived*
> *At another's beck and call: their money goes*
> *Wasted on Babylonian coverlets....**

Or to a robe, or dresses....

---

* Embroidered Babylonian coverlets—ostensibly fancy couch covers—were an extremely big deal in ancient Rome. The Emperor Nero once bought one for 4 million sesterces (approximately $200,000 in today's U.S. currency).

Friedrich Nietzsche
(1844–1900)

"Ah, women. They make the highs higher and the lows more frequent."

German philosopher Friedrich Nietzsche was a lifelong bachelor whose misogynistic ranting did not dissuade women from approaching him. "Because his philosophy bore the reputation of being blasphemous and indecent, he was quite a hero in the pump rooms and on the piazzas of many watering places," journalist H. L. Mencken wrote. Nietzsche failed to capitalize on his opportunities for romance, however, choosing to direct his affection toward women who were disinterested in him.

Nietzsche first fell in love at the age of thirty-two with Mat Hilde Trampedach. After their second encounter, Nietzsche sent her a marriage proposal in the mail. "Will you become my wife? I love you and I feel as if you already belong to me. . . . Do you not believe as I do that in a union each will become freer and better than in singleness? Well then, excelsior." Trampedach, already in love with another man, declined. Nietzsche's libido shrunk into hiding for the next five years.

In 1882, Nietzsche met the twenty-one-year-old Russian Lou von Salomé in Zurich. He wrote that "she is plain . . . but like all plain girls, she has cultivated her mind in order to be attractive." While Nietzsche the philosopher captivated her, Nietzsche the lover was less than compelling—Salomé turned down multiple marriage offers from him. Nietzsche's sister Elisabeth wrote an angry letter to Salomé defending her brother's wounded pride. Salomé replied, "Don't think that I have any designs upon your brother or that I am in love with him; I could sleep in the same room with him and not have any thoughts of arousal."

When Salomé became engaged to another man several years later, Nietzsche told a friend that he wished her "much happiness and prosperity," although he refused to write to her: "One must keep out of the way of the kind of creature who does not understand awe and respect." Their mutual friend Paul Rée was amused by the whole situation, remarking that he did not see how Salomé could have kissed Nietzsche with the philosopher's bushy mustache in the way.

Nietzsche once claimed in jest that he had never touched a woman. In truth, he engaged in intercourse on several occasions "on doctor's orders." Unfortunately, a stable relationship with a woman was not meant to be. "For me to marry," Nietzsche wrote, "would probably be sheer asininity."

In his later years, Nietzsche descended into madness as the result of a syphilitic infection, which very probably stemmed from his doctor-ordered encounters. Nietzsche was originally treated for syphilis in his early twenties and suffered from chronic health problems—poor eyesight, headaches, vomiting, and fatigue—in the intervening years that were further evidence of infection.*

On January 3, 1889, Nietzsche experienced a severe psychotic break on the streets of Turin. After witnessing a horse being whipped, he threw his arms around the beast and collapsed at its feet. Two policemen arrived on the scene to find Nietzsche babbling and incoherent. He never recovered his sanity during the final eleven years of his life.

IN HIS OWN WORDS
The Great Repression

Nietzsche vehemently criticized the Victorian era's repression of all things sexual. "The church fights passion by cutting it out, in every sense; its practice, its therapy, is *castration*," he wrote. "It was Christianity, on the basis of its *resentment against* life, that first made something unclean out of sexuality." Ironic sentiments for a man whose health continually suffered due to the lingering effects of a sexually transmitted disease.

---

* His friend Richard Wagner suggested that Nietzsche's health problems were caused by excessive masturbation. "Wagner is full of malicious ideas," Nietzsche said when his condition temporarily improved. "I took myself in hand, I made myself healthy again." It is unclear whether the pun was intentional.

Plato
(c. 427–c. 347 BC)

"Love is a serious mental disease."

Few details are known about Greek philosopher Plato's love life except that he died a lifelong bachelor at the age of eighty-one. Fortunately, he left ample material on the relations between men and women—much of which appears disturbing to the modern reader.

Take his idea of Utopia, as laid out in *The Republic*. In contrast to the modern concept of a utopia as a paradise or Heaven on Earth, Plato's Utopia is a city run by the iron fist of the State. In Plato's Utopia, marriages are arranged by the State based upon eugenic ideals. If "inferior" couples had children, the kids would be "put away in some mysterious unknown place, as they ought to be." The children of the State-sponsored "superior" couples would also be taken away from their parents to be raised by the community; no children would ever know their parents, nor their parents them. Children would call every elder that they met "mother" or "father" and everyone of a similar age "brother" or "sister."

To avoid the problems associated with private property, wives would not belong solely to their husbands. Instead, "women shall be, without exception, the common wives of . . . men, and no one shall have a wife of his own." How this "common" arrangement

would affect the State-sponsored breeding program is unclear, although Plato makes it clear that women outside of the age range
of twenty to forty who found themselves pregnant would be required to have abortions—or commit infanticide.

While there was no room for romance in Plato's Utopia,
there was plenty of room for war. Boys and girls who showed
an aptitude for fighting would be trained from an early age to
be warriors; if they exhibited no skill for the art of war, a State-
enforced division of labor would assist them in choosing a career path. The main goal of the Utopia was to achieve military
superiority over states that would threaten its well-being and
maybe enough food to feed the masses. Philosopher Bertrand
Russell (page 134) wrote:

> Skill in war and enough to eat is all that will be achieved.
> Plato had lived through famine and defeat in Athens;
> perhaps, subconsciously, he thought the avoidance of
> these evils the best that statesmanship could accomplish.

NOT IN HIS OWN WORDS
Platonic Love

Today, the term "platonic love" is used to refer to intimate, non-
sexual friendships, usually between heterosexual members of

the opposite sex. The opinions of the characters in Plato's dialogues, by contrast, are often contradictory. In his masterworks *Phaedrus* and *Symposium*, Plato paints a picture of love that is both physical and spiritual in nature. Plato identified the various forms of love as the love of God, the love of flesh, the love of self, and the love of friend, the last of which gave rise to the modern-day idea of "platonic love."

Ayn Rand
(1905–1982)

*"To say 'I love you' one must first know
how to say the 'I.'"*

Russian-American Ayn Rand, best known for her philosophical novels *Atlas Shrugged* and *The Fountainhead*, believed that in order to love another person, one must first love oneself. Based upon the sordid details of her romantic life, Rand clearly loved herself with abandon.

In 1955, after establishing herself as a bestselling novelist, the fifty-year-old (and married) Rand began a workplace romance with twenty-five-year-old Nathaniel Branden. After Branden wrote her a fan letter in 1950, Rand and her husband, Frank O'Connor, met with Branden and his fiancée Barbara. The foursome quickly formed a tight-knit intellectual friendship; when Nathaniel and Barbara married, Rand and O'Connor stood up for them as maid of honor and best man.

Despite the twenty-five-year gulf separating Branden and herself, Rand recognized in him a kindred philosophical spirit. Their shared belief in personal liberty, laissez-faire capitalism, and rationalism led them to cofound the "Objectivist" school of thought. Their movement rejected spirituality and altruism, instead praising reason and self-interest as the highest values. As Rand groomed Branden to be the "intellectual heir" to her life's work, they inadvertently fell in love.

But this was no ordinary clandestine affair: After disclosing their feelings to each other, Rand and Branden pitched the idea of an affair to Branden's wife Barbara. While Branden insisted that his feelings for Rand did not in any way change how he felt about Barbara, his wife's "visibly dazed state" made it clear that things were Not Okay.* When Rand's husband Frank walked in on the trio, Rand proceeded to explain their proposal to him with

> the persistence of a drill cutting through granite. After Barbara and Frank flared up in angry protest, Ayn became still warmer, gentler, and more implacable. She acknowledged their feelings, conveyed compassion for their pain, and tried to make them accept the situation with the single-mindedness of a military commander.

The oddest part of their talk is that, at this time, all they were proposing was an *emotional* affair. "It's not as if we were proposing a sexual relationship," Rand said. They wished only

---

* A note to prospective adulterers: While seeking your spouse's permission to stray may sound courteous, it is no less disrespectful. Branden himself later acknowledged this. "Ayn's and my cruelty did not lie in falling in love or even, primarily, in pursuing an affair. The cruelty lay in how we dealt with the matter: our lack of genuine compassion for Frank and Barbara's predicament," he said.

to meet a few times a week, in private, to "talk." Their spouses reluctantly agreed to the arrangement.

To no one's surprise, Rand and Branden began sleeping together five months later.

"She made love with the same single-tracked concentration with which she did everything else," Branden wrote. The sexual intensity of their relationship distracted Rand from her in-progress novel *Atlas Shrugged*. "Have you been sent by the enemy to prevent me from finishing this book?" she asked Branden. She eventually finished her masterpiece in 1957, dedicating it to both her husband and her young lover.

Branden and his wife finally separated in 1965, but here the plot thickens: He was secretly seeing a beautiful young fashion model, Patrecia Scott. Rand was unaware of his affair with Scott but could feel Branden pulling away from her emotionally. "The man to whom I dedicated *Atlas Shrugged* would never want anything less than me! I don't care if I'm ninety years old and in a wheelchair!" she berated him.

When Branden revealed his relationship with Patrecia to Rand, the older woman went ballistic. Rand, deeming him unfit to continue his role as her intellectual heir, publicly exiled Branden from the Objectivist movement that they had built together. "You would have been nothing without me," she screamed in a fit of rage, "and you will be nothing when I'm done with you!" She had his name removed from the dedication page of subsequent printings of *Atlas Shrugged* and tried to block publication of Branden's own book, *The Psychology of Self-Help*.*

Rand's husband stood stoically by her side during the fallout with Branden, and, despite its ups and down, their marriage lasted over fifty years until Frank's death in 1979.

IN HER OWN WORDS
Love As I Say, Not As I Do

Rand tiptoed around the issue of infidelity in a 1964 *Playboy* interview with Alvin Toffler. "I consider promiscuity immoral. Not because sex is evil, but because sex is too good and too important." When she was asked if only married partners should have sex, she said:

> Not necessarily. What sex should involve is a very serious relationship. . . . I consider marriage a very important institution . . . [but] either [married or unmarried sex] is moral, provided only that both parties take the relationship seriously and that it is based on values.

---

* Despite Rand's attempted interference, *The Psychology of Self-Help* was successfully published and sold over a million copies worldwide. Branden would later pen *The Psychology of Romantic Love* and *The Romantic Love Question & Answer Book*.

Jean-Jacques Rousseau
(1712–1778)

*"What is true love itself if it is not illusion?
If we saw what we love exactly as it is,
there would be no more love on earth."*

French Enlightenment philosopher Jean-Jacques Rousseau believed that humankind's natural state had been corrupted by society. "Man is born free; and everywhere he is in chains," he wrote. "But human nature does not go backward, and we never return to the times of innocence and equality, when we have once departed from them." Political instruments such as marriage are necessary "chains" that we must voluntarily submit to. The nuclear family—built around the core of a husband and wife—is integral to the cohesiveness of society.

His private life could not have been any further from his publicly stated philosophies: Rousseau engaged in many romantic relationships and ignored his filial responsibilities when they arose. The nuclear family, that necessary straitjacket that all men must wear, did not fit Rousseau.

In his autobiography, he recounted his relationships with upper-class women such as Madame de Larange, Madame de Savoy, and Madame de Warens. The noblewoman Warens took him into her home where Rousseau lived with her and the steward of her house in an illicit *ménage a trois*. Rousseau considered Warens the love of his life, but they eventually parted ways when he took a job in another city.

Despite his dalliances with high society, Rousseau's longest relationship was with Thérèse Levasseur, an illiterate seamstress whom he met in March 1745. They had five children together, a sizable family . . . or it would have been, if they had kept any of their offspring: Rousseau personally abandoned every one of their five children to a French foundling hospital (sort of like a YMCA for unwanted children). The kids would have otherwise interfered with Rousseau's important philosophical work, he argued.

Neither Rousseau nor Levasseur were faithful to each other, but after abandoning their fifth and final child in 1768, they decided to marry. The marriage was not legal, though, as unions between Catholics (Rousseau) and Protestants (Levasseur) were not recognized in France at the time. That appeared to be fine with Rousseau, who barely acknowledged Levasseur anyway: Instead of referring to her as his wife, he preferred to call her his "housekeeper." He kept her "services" until his death in 1778.

IN HIS OWN WORDS
Spank You Very Much

Rousseau's sexual proclivities were thoroughly documented in *Confessions*, his posthumously published autobiography. His appetites were in stark contrast to the conventional moral code that he championed in his philosophical writings, the most salacious passages featuring candid admissions of his various fetishes, including masochism, spanking, and flashing.

On S&M:

To fall at the feet of an imperious mistress, obey her mandates, or implore pardon, were for me the most exquisite enjoyments, and the more my blood was inflamed by the efforts of a lively imagination the more I acquired the appearance of a whining lover.

On spanking:

[My governess Miss Lambercier] had often threatened [us with spanking], and this threat of a treatment entirely new, appeared to me extremely dreadful; but after the execution, I found it much less terrible than the idea, and what is peculiar, this punishment increased my affection for the person who had inflicted it. . . . Who would believe this childish discipline, received at eight years old, from the hands of a woman of 30, should influence my propensities, my desires, my passions, for the rest of my life, and that in quite a contrary sense from what might naturally have been expected?

On flashing:

I haunted dark alleys and lonely spots where I could expose myself to women. . . . The absurd pleasure I got from displaying myself before their eyes is quite indescribable. . . . The more sensible pretended that they had seen nothing. Others started laughing.

Bertrand Russell
(1872–1970)

*"Marriage is for most women the commonest
mode of livelihood, and the total amount of
undesired sex endured by women is probably
greater in marriage than in prostitution."*

Bertrand Russell was an Englishman of many talents, working alternately as a philosopher, a logician, a mathematician, a social reformer, and a historian. His *History of Western Philosophy* provided a foundation for all future philosophy surveys (including this book). Russell won the Nobel Prize in Literature in 1950 "in recognition of his varied and significant writings in which he champions humanitarian ideals and freedom of thought." And, if such an award existed, he would have also been awarded the medal for Most Marriages by a Renowned Philosopher.

Russell believed that bad marriages were especially destructive to creative types (such as himself): "When [an artist] is compelled by fear of social and economic persecution to go on living in a marriage which has become intolerable, he is deprived of the energy which artistic creation requires." He argued passionately for the right to divorce, likening a bad marriage to a prison. Over his lifetime, Russell broke free from three such matrimonial prisons.

At the age of twenty-two, he married Alys Pearsall Smith (Wife No. 1). Their union lasted nearly twenty-seven years.

Next, he married Dora Winifred Black (Wife No. 2) in 1921. This was an open marriage: both partners were free to engage in sexual relations outside of their marriage. When Dora became pregnant by another man in 1935, Russell considered their pact broken and divorced her. One year later, he married Patricia "Peter" Spence (Wife No. 3) . . . and divorced *her* in 1952.

Russell also engaged in adulterous relationships with at least two married women. He believed that, as long as the relationship is "profoundly important" and there are no children to be affected, adultery should not be subject to criminal, civic, or public condemnation. Russell did not regret his time spent with various women. As he wrote in *Autobiography*:

> It seems to me that men need women, and women need men, mentally as much as physically. For my part, I owe a great deal to women whom I have loved, and without them I should have been far more narrow-minded.

Russell lived his life for three things: "the longing for love, the search for knowledge, and unbearable pity for the suffering of mankind." After a lifetime of searching, he at last found lasting love: When he was eighty, he settled down for good with Edith Finch (Wife No. 4). Although she was thirty years his junior, they had known each other for over twenty-five years. "Though it might seem too good for human life, this is what—

at last—I have found." He lived with Finch until he died at the age of ninety-eight.

IN HIS OWN WORDS
Ah, Youth

Marriage and Morals, published in 1929, summarized Russell's early thoughts on the subject of marriage. He foresaw a future where fathers were less important as the heads of household. With fathers out of the way and single mothers roaming the earth, Russell believed that governments would take over the education and welfare of citizens, thereby paving the way for the complete collapse of Western civilization.

Three divorces and some fifty years later, he admitted to erring in his judgment:

I do not know what I think now about the subject of marriage. . . . Perhaps easy divorce causes less unhappiness than any other system, but I am no longer capable of being dogmatic on the subject of marriage.

Jean-Paul Sartre
(1905–1980)

"There are of course ugly women,
but I prefer those who are pretty."

French existentialist Jean-Paul Sartre was an unlikely candidate for a "literary Don Juan" (as he liked to call himself). The first girl that he became infatuated with in school rejected him, calling him a "cross-eyed old fool." It was an inauspicious introduction to the opposite sex. His prospects did not look any more promising as an adult: He stood just five-foot-one, dressed in oversized clothes, and had no concept of personal hygiene.

Sartre miraculously overcame these deficiencies by simply ignoring them and projecting an aura of confidence. He admitted that, as a youth, "[I] was very melancholy because I was ugly and that made me suffer. I have absolutely rid myself of that, because it's a weakness." He only needed one thing to seduce women: *les mots* ("his words").

He lost his virginity at the age of eighteen to an older married woman. "I did it with no great enthusiasm," he said, "because she wasn't very pretty." It was okay for *him* to be ugly, but Sartre held the women he slept with to a higher standard. In a similar vein, he felt no respect for prostitutes because "a girl shouldn't give herself like that" . . . yet he regularly visited brothels with his university friends.

When Sartre was twenty-one, he fell in love with Germaine Marron and requested her hand in marriage. Her parents originally consented but called the wedding off when Sartre failed his teaching exam in the summer of 1928. "I was relieved," Sartre wrote. "I'm not sure of having acted quite correctly in this whole affair."

In fact, he had not been acting "correctly" during his engagement: He had been having an affair with Simone Jollivet, a playwright and actress who lived in the nearby city of Toulouse. When Sartre presented Jollivet with a bottle of perfume, he was miffed that she placed it on her nightstand beside four other bottles from four other lovers. "What? Do you own me?" she said angrily. "Am I supposed to sit here and wait for your *occasional* appearances [in Toulouse]?" After thinking it over, Sartre agreed with her. "She was right, of course, and I knew it. I concluded that jealousy *is* possessiveness. *Therefore*, I decided never to be jealous again."

In 1929, while studying for his second attempt at his teaching certification, Sartre met a fellow philosophy student who shared his values: Simone de Beauvoir. The long and winding road from their meeting to their burial in a shared Parisian grave is recounted earlier in this book (page 31), but suffice it to say that the open nature of their relationship allowed Sartre the freedom to sleep around as he pleased. His burgeoning literary fame—as a playwright, novelist, screenwriter, and critic—guaranteed him a constant stream of young ladies who were eager to make his acquaintance.

Sartre's love life was not without drama. He often saw several different women concurrently, booking them into separate slots in his busy schedule. (It's amazing that he ever found the time to write.) The details of his various liaisons is dizzying, but here's a taste from Hazel Rowley's Sartre-Beauvoir biography *Tête-à-Tête*:

> His women all lived within ten minutes of him; they rarely saw one another, and none of them knew the truth about his life. Arlette had no idea that after going for three weeks' vacation every year with *her*, Sartre went away with Wanda for two or three weeks. Wanda did not know that Sartre still saw Michelle. When he slept at Beauvoir's, he told Wanda he was sleeping at home. His letters to Wanda were filled with outrageous inventions. He'd be late back to Paris, he once told her. He was locked up in a castle in Austria.

He continued to live out his promiscuous dream right until the end of his life. In 1979, at the age of seventy-four, a toothless and blind Sartre remarked to one of his girlfriends that, not counting Beauvoir and her girlfriend Sylvie Le Bon, "there are nine women in my life at the moment!" Not a bad ending for a "cross-eyed old fool."

IN HIS OWN WORDS
Sartre's Crabs

When he was thirty-two, Jean-Paul Sartre was plagued by a bad case of crabs. As he told John Gerassi in 1971:

> After I took mescaline, I started seeing crabs around me all the time. [Three or four of them] followed me in the streets, into class. I got used to them. I would wake up in the morning and say, "Good morning, my little ones, how did you sleep?" I would talk to them all the time. I would say, "Okay, guys, we're going into class now, so we have to be still and quiet," and they would be there, around my desk, absolutely still, until the bell rang. . . . The crabs stayed with me until the day I simply decided that they bored me and that I just wouldn't pay attention to them.

Arthur Schopenhauer
(1788–1860)

*"Love is only the species' will for survival,
the need to propagate the species."*

The great German pessimist Arthur Schopenhauer knew exactly what he wanted in a woman. "A certain plumpness . . . [and] a full female bosom has an uncommon charm."* Unfortunately, he believed that he did not have what women were looking for in exchange. According to Schopenhauer, all women want a man

> thirty to thirty-five years of age. . . . Lack of brains is of no consequence to a woman; rather, excessive mental power, or even genius, being an abnormality, may operate unfavorably. Therefore, we often see an ugly, stupid, and rude man cut out a well-bred, talented, and amiable man.

In the end, it meant little to Schopenhauer, because all romantic affairs are doomed anyway. "After he has finally obtained satisfaction, every lover will experience a wonderful

---

* The large breasts were not for Schopenhauer, but for his children: An ample bosom "promises the newly born plenty of nourishment."

disappointment," Schopenhauer wrote. "After the final completion of the great work, [every lover] finds himself deceived: for the illusion has vanished."

He "completed" at least one great work, fathering a child with a maid in Dresden. There's no historical record of the woman's or child's names—we know about them only from letters that Schopenhauer sent to his sister. Their relationship was apparently confined to a one-night stand. His daughter died as an infant in 1819, and he never saw the maid again. (Although this was the only child he was to have, Schopenhauer believed that "a man can conveniently beget more than a hundred children a year, if as many women were at his disposal.")

In 1821, the thirty-year-old philosopher began seeing a nineteen-year-old opera singer, Caroline Richter, an affair notable because she was one of the few women who returned his affections. Schopenhauer sabotaged their relationship with his dim views of marriage, which gave new meaning to "fear of commitment": "Marrying means to halve one's rights and double one's duties." Needless to say, Caroline left Schopenhauer.

In what would be his final attempt at romance, Schopenhauer at age forty-three turned his attentions to seventeen-year-old Flora Weiss. He approached her at a party bearing a bunch of grapes (apparently roses were out of the price range for a part-time philosopher). The feelings were not mutual: As Flora recorded in her diary, "I didn't want the grapes because old Schopenhauer had touched them."

Schopenhauer, lonely and bitter, longed for the "restoration of woman to her rightful and natural position, the subordinate one." Mankind can't expect too much from the fairer sex. "The most eminent heads of the entire sex have proved incapable of a single truly great, genuine and original achievement in art, or indeed of creating anything at all of lasting value," he wrote in his masterpiece of misogyny, *On Women*. "We can say that by candidly publishing such sentiments before the whole world, he was not helping his chances [with women]," philosophical lecturer Alexander S. Rosenthal said.

Schopenhauer died alone in 1860. Perhaps it is for the best that he never married. While he was unhappy being single, he predicted that he would have been far more miserable in matrimony.

> When gratified, [marriages] lead more often to unhappiness than to happiness. For its demands often conflict so strongly with the personal welfare of the interested. . . . [After having children, love] vanishes and leaves behind a hated companion for life. "Who marries for love must live in grief," says the Spanish proverb.

IN HIS OWN WORDS
Jack and Jill Went Up a Hill . . .

Arthur Schopenhauer contemplated love only with great reluctance, as a dearth of philosophical inquiry into the subject *forced* him to contemplate it. "One ought rather to wonder that a matter which plays such an important part throughout human life, has been hitherto scarcely at all taken into consideration by philosophers," Schopenhauer wrote.

> Next to love of life, [romantic love] proves the strongest and most active of all incentives; continually engages half the powers and thoughts of the younger portion of humanity; is the last goal of almost every human endeavor; gains influence over the most important affairs; interrupts at every hour the most serious occupations; unbalances at times even the greatest minds. . . . Nothing is at stake but that every Jack may find his Jill; why should such a trifle play so important a part, and unceasingly bring disturbance and confusion into the well-regulated affairs of life?

Seneca the Younger
(c. 4 BC–AD 65)

"Friendship always benefits; love sometimes injures."

Roman philosopher Seneca the Younger* was banished from Rome in AD 41 on charges of adultery with the Emperor Claudius's niece, Julia Livilla, proving that love does in fact sometimes injure. (This is especially true when that love is between a forty-year-old man and a twenty-year-old married princess.)

After living in exile on the island of Corsica for eight years, Seneca returned in 49 at the behest of the emperor's wife (and Julia's sister), Agrippina. In 50, Seneca married a wealthy woman, Pompeia Paulina, and began tutoring Agrippina's son Nero. When Nero assumed the Roman throne in 54, Seneca became his political adviser.

Nero's tumultuous fourteen-year rule on the throne was marked by paranoia and persecution—among other atrocities, he executed his own mother, Agrippina. Seneca could not control the emperor and stood in silent witness to his reign of terror before retiring from his post after eight years of service.

---

* His father Seneca the Elder was a writer as well, but the younger Seneca did not wish to capitalize on his father's accomplishments. "He who boasts of his ancestry, praises the deeds of another," Seneca the Younger wrote.

After Seneca admitted to plotting to overthrow the emperor in 65, Nero ordered the philosopher and his co-conspirators to commit suicide. According to Roman historian Tacitus, Seneca told his wife not to allow his death

> to be a permanent burden; rather to take genuine consolation for the loss of her husband in the contemplation of his virtuous life. Paulina assured him that she had every intention of dying with him, and demanded a share of the fatal knife. Seneca, by no means averse to her having her moment of glory . . . said: "I offered you the comfort of life: you have chosen the dignity of death. I shall not deny you the chance to show such an example." . . . Then they sliced open the veins in their arms with a single stroke of the knife.

Seneca had already withered away from fasting and had a difficult time getting the blood to flow from his wrists. He asked his wife, who was bleeding from her own wounds, to leave the room. Seneca then asked his doctor to administer a poison to him to speed up his death; the poison also failed to kill him. He was next placed into a hot bath where the steam finally suffocated him.

Nero, meanwhile, heard that Paulina had slit her wrists, and he ordered her arms to be bandaged and for doctors to keep her alive. She survived her suicide attempt, but was "faithful to her husband's memory to a most praiseworthy degree, the pallor of her face and body testifying to the extent to which her soul had been destroyed."

IN HIS OWN WORDS
Bet You Can't Have Just One

Seneca the Younger satirized the relaxed morals that he saw as poisoning the well of Roman society:

> Can any one feel ashamed of adultery, now that things have come to such a pass that no woman keeps a husband at all unless it be to pique her lover? Chastity merely implies ugliness. Where will you find any woman so abject, so repulsive, as to be satisfied with a single pair of lovers, without having a different one for each hour of the day; nor is the day long enough for all of them, unless she has taken her airing in the grounds of one, and passes the night with another.

Despite being a work of satire, it is difficult to read his words here without being reminded of the cause of his exile.

Socrates
(469–399 BC)

*"By all means, marry. If you get a good wife,
you'll become happy; if you get a bad one,
you'll become a philosopher."*

The Greek philosopher Socrates was a squat man with a snub nose and projecting eyes. He wandered the streets of Athens, engaging strangers in random philosophical conversations. Despite his odd appearance and behavior, Socrates was well known and liked throughout the Greek city-state.* A bachelor for most of his life, he finally married when he was in his fifties or sixties.

His wife, the fiery Xanthippe, was, by some accounts, up to forty years younger than Socrates. In stark contrast to the submissive lives that women were expected to lead in ancient Greece, Xanthippe publicly berated her elderly husband. According to one legend, after a heated verbal exchange between the couple, Xanthippe poured dirty water from a pail onto her husband's head. Socrates knew that he had it coming to him, joking that "it generally rains after thunder."

Socrates took his wife's behavior in stride. "As I intended to associate with all kinds of people, I thought nothing they could

---

* Until a jury of his peers sentenced him to death.

do would disturb me, once I had accustomed myself to bear the disposition of Xanthippe," he said. Xanthippe's reputation as a nagging wife is now permanently embedded in the history books: Shakespeare invoked her name as a "curst and shrewd" woman in *The Taming of the Shrew*.*

In 399 BC, Socrates was put on trial for corrupting the youth of Athens with his philosophy. He disputed the spurious charges at his trial but refused to beg for mercy. He even promised to continue practicing philosophy should the court find him not guilty. The jury convicted him and sentenced him to death.

Faced with the prospect of raising their three children alone, Xanthippe was understandably upset. On the day that Socrates' sentence was to be carried out, she wept profusely in front of his friends who were visiting him. "Please let someone take her home," Socrates said to his friend Criton. All other women were banished from his bedside; Socrates believed that a deathbed was no place for mourning. Surrounded by his male friends and students, he drank a cup of hemlock, a poisonous European plant.

Tears started flowing down his usually stoic friends' faces. "You are strange fellows; what is wrong with you?" the in-

---

* Socrates' wife's name has become so synonymous with "shrew" that there is now an actual species of shrew named after her: Xanthippe's shrew (*Crocidura xantippe*) can be found in eastern Africa.

credulous Socrates said. "I sent the women away for this very purpose, to stop their creating such a scene. I have heard that one should die in silence. So please be quiet and keep control of yourselves." Socrates walked around to allow the poison to work its way through his system, finally lying down when his extremities started going numb. He directed his last words to Criton: "We owe a cock to Asclepius. Do pay it. Don't forget."

IN HIS OWN WORDS
He's Just Not That Into You

Over the course of several meetings, the Athenian youth Alcibiades tried to seduce the elder Socrates. While Socrates was no stranger to sleeping with young men, he had no interest in engaging in physical activity with this particular youth—even when they wrestled each other in the nude, Socrates remained unaroused. "I came to realize that he was far more invulnerable in every way to bribery than Ajax had been to the sword," Alcibiades said.

Socrates gently chided the boy, believing that Alcibiades did not possess the maturity to appreciate the older philosopher's intellect:

You must perceive in me a sort of incredible beauty, but of a kind I mean, very different from your own good looks. . . . [You wish to] make a trade—beauty for beauty—well! . . . That's really the old "gold-for-bronze" exchange!

Emanuel Swedenborg
(1688–1772)

"Man knows that love is, but not what it is."

I t is quite understandable that Swedish philosopher Emanuel Swedenborg knew "not what love is": Over the course of his eighty-four years, he had zero experience with it.

The lifelong bachelor passed his time on Earth by writing about love, marriage, and—perhaps unsurprisingly—the subject of sexual frustration. Swedenborg believed that thwarted sexual impulses did more harm to society than premarital sex, since

> with some men the love of the sex cannot without harm
> be restrained from going forth into fornication. There is
> no need to recount the injuries which excessive restraint
> of the love of [women] may cause with those who . . .
> suffer from intense venereal excitement.*

---

* Swedenborg was likely writing about either *vasocongestion* or *priapism*. Vasocongestion (or "blue balls") is a painful but harmless buildup of fluid in the testicles and prostate brought on by prolonged sexual arousal. While blue balls may be uncomfortable and require release, the condition is not known to cause "injuries." Priapism, on the other hand, is a persistent pe-

His own repressed urges led to vivid erotic dreams, which he recorded in a diary from 1743 to 1744. One of his more lurid dreams involved a *ménage à trois* with two women, one older and one younger than him. Which woman should he make love to first? Swedenborg believed the dream represented a dilemma that he faced in his writing: Should he continue with his older, intellectual work or go down a new, spiritual path? He chose the younger woman, thus deciding the direction of his theological studies.

The fifty-six-year-old Swedenborg dove headfirst into his new spiritual endeavor, believing that he could speak to dead people. He started carrying out full conversations with the dearly departed, the elaborate hallucinations that fueled his writing. "I am well aware that many will say that no one can possibly speak with spirits and angels as long as he lives in the body," he wrote.

Swedenborg published his divinely inspired riffs on love in his bestseller *Conjugal Love*. (He defined "conjugal love" as "spiritual love.") Unlike other theologians, he embraced the concept of premarital sex. "The spiritual is in fact actually evolved out of the natural, and when the spiritual has been evolved, then the natural compasses it about as bark does the

---

nile erection lasting for four or more hours. This rare condition is triggered by certain diseases and drugs (e.g., Viagra). If left untreated, priapism may result in permanent tissue death.

wood and as the sheath the sword."* Besides, he argued, earthly marriage has one specific goal: Reproduction in order to fill Heaven with new citizens. Although premarital sex should be discouraged, Heaven can always use more angels.

On his deathbed, Swedenborg was witnessed talking to angels in the room with him as if they were living people. A pastor asked him why no one else could see the spirits. The eighty-four-year-old virgin replied that it was because most people are "so carnally minded." The angels graced Swedenborg with their presence because of his chastity of both body and mind.

IN HIS OWN WORDS
The Joy of Angel Sex

Emanuel Swedenborg's direct line to God allowed him to observe something that few mortals are privy to: the bedroom habits of angels.

Marriage, it turns out, does not end when Death Do We Part. Swedenborg wrote that "husbands who have loved their wives, in case they die, are desirous to know whether it be well with them, and whether they shall ever meet again." Married couples *do* meet up in Heaven, and if their love is "good and

---

* No puns intended—Swedenborg was above such juvenile tomfoolery.

true," they can continue to live together as man and wife, enjoying "similar communication with each other as in the world, but more delightful and blessed" (i.e., no more arguments over trivial matters such as dishes and yard work). If a couple continues to feud in the spiritual realm (for whatever reason), that is easily remedied: A new angel spouse will be provided.

Heavenly love between the sexes consists not of carnal pleasures but of "celestial sweets." A Real Angel Bearing a Trumpet told Swedenborg that sex exists "in the heavens, as on earth; but only with those in the heavens who are in the marriage of good and truth."

Henry David Thoreau
(1817–1862)

*"If common sense had been consulted,
how many marriages would never
have taken place?"*

American naturalist Henry David Thoreau lived a simple life in and near the woods, where he was free from the trivialities of modern society. "The mind can be permanently profaned by the habit of attending to trivial things, so that all our thoughts shall be tinged with triviality," he wrote.*

For a naturalist, Thoreau's views on sexuality were surprisingly conservative. "Love and lust are far asunder," he wrote. "The one is good, the other bad." In a perfect world, sex would be "treated naturally and simply . . . [as] there is far more purity, as well as more impurity, than is apparent." Pure love, when founded on mutual respect, elevates base pleasure to "loftier delights."

Such mutual delights would not come easily for Thoreau. He was ideally suited for solitary living since he was "as ugly as sin, long-nosed, queer-mouthed, and with uncouth and rustic, though courteous, manners, corresponding very well with [his] exterior," according to neighbor Nathaniel Hawthorne. Thoreau's "uncouth" manners included eating with his hands, rarely bathing, and wearing shabby clothes.

---

* We can only imagine what he would have to say about Facebook.

In 1839, Thoreau and his brother John both fell in love with the same girl, family friend Ellen Sewall. Her father, a Unitarian minister, did not approve of either of the young Thoreau boys. John proposed to Ellen first; she rejected him. Henry tried his hand next, proposing to her in a letter. Although the letter has not survived, a journal entry dated November 1, 1840, likely used similar language: "I thought that the sun of our love should have risen as noiselessly as the sun out of the sea." In spite of its flowery prose (or perhaps because of it), Henry's marriage proposal also met with a swift refusal.

Following the rejected proposal, Henry wrote, "Love is the profoundest of secrets. Divulged, even to the beloved, it is no longer Love." He was infatuated with other women throughout his life, but he never fell in love again. He wrote that it is "rare, indeed, that we meet with one to whom we are prepared to be quite ideally related, as she to us." Thoreau never married because, in his mind at least, Sewall was "the one" for him.

IN HIS OWN WORDS
Thoroughly Modern Henry

Some scholars have theorized that Thoreau was a repressed homosexual. "No biographical study of the writer is complete without addressing the likelihood that even while in the forest,

Thoreau was in the closet," *Boise Weekly* columnist Nicholas Collias wrote. Thoreau had a fondness for watching nude male swimmers, maintained a large library of homoerotic classical literature, and wrote sexually charged journal entries about muscular male bodies and phallic-shaped plants. His "actions and words . . . indicate a specific sexual interest in members of his own sex," scholar Walter Harding wrote in the aptly named *Journal of Homosexuality*.

Leo Tolstoy
(1828–1910)

"Love does not exist. There exists the physical need for intercourse, and the rational need for a mate in life."

Russian author Leo Tolstoy's first sexual experience was with a prostitute when he was just fourteen years old. His brother took him to a brothel to inaugurate Tolstoy into manhood. After having sex with the prostitute, Tolstoy broke down in tears—an inauspicious introduction to sexuality that would set the tone for the rest of his life.

His first adult relationship was with a twenty-three-year-old serf, Aksinya Alexandrovna Bazykina. Tolstoy, by then in his twenties, wrote that he was "in love as never before." He became very attached to Aksinya, but marriage between a master and a serf was not a legitimate option in Russian society. (Never mind the fact that she was already married.) They had a child together, Timofei, whom he never publicly acknowledged.

Still, Tolstoy longed for a family of his own. "I must get married this year—or not at all," Tolstoy's New Year's resolution from 1859 read. The year passed without any wedding bells. Then, in 1862, when he was thirty-four, a trio of sisters piqued his interest. His first choice of wife was the youngest sister, Tatyana. Their mother would not relinquish the sixteen-year-old to Tolstoy—she wanted Liza, the oldest sister, married off first. Tolstoy was unimpressed with Liza. "How beautifully unhappy she would be if she were my wife," Tolstoy wrote.

Tolstoy made a novel compromise: He proposed to the middle sister, Sophia Andreevna Behrs. She was "plain and vulgar" to his eyes but attractive nonetheless. He told Sophia that her youth and vivacity made him all too aware of his own age and "incapacity for happiness." While this was clearly a terrible pickup line, his interest in her was enough to set Sophia's heart aflutter. "They were not even sufficiently well-acquainted to know whether they *liked* one another. Probably they never did," biographer A. N. Wilson wrote. "He found her strange and fascinating. She found him monstrous and frightening."

On their wedding day, Tolstoy showed his diaries to his bride, revealing his world of prostitutes, promiscuity, gonorrhea, and homoerotic thoughts in unflinching detail. "I don't think I ever recovered from the shock of reading the diaries when I was engaged to him," Sophia wrote years later. "I can still remember the agonizing pangs of jealousy." Sophia cried the rest of the day, including throughout their wedding ceremony. After the service, when she hugged her mother, Tolstoy chastised her: "If leaving your family means such great sorrow to you, then you cannot love me very much."

While he believed that chastity was man's ideal state, sex within marriage for the explicit purpose of procreation was a close second (i.e., no birth control for the Tolstoys). Famous for massive novels such as the four-volume, 1,225-page brick

War and Peace, Tolstoy set about building an equally impressive family: The couple would have a total of thirteen children, of which only eight survived childhood. Thankfully, his books sold well, allowing his entire family to live comfortably on a large estate.

The couple had their fair share of arguments over the years, most of which were recounted in gruesome detail in Sophia's diaries and in Tolstoy's thinly veiled autobiographical novels. Their troubles were only heightened when, toward the end of his life, Tolstoy became fanatically religious and swore off his earthly existence. He moved into a hut on his family's property while his wife and children continued to live in their mansion. When he tried to renounce copyright to all of his works, Sophia went ballistic—she needed the income from his works to support their family. Sophia was unwilling to accept her husband's callousness. "I want to kill myself, to fall in love with someone—anything only not to live with the man whom I have loved all my life," she wrote. Her various suicide attempts and threats included poisoning (opium, ammonia), lying down on train tracks, throwing herself into a well, and freezing herself to death in a bed of snow in the dead of winter. She never succeeded. Tolstoy was unmoved by his wife's actions. "If anyone would wish to drown, it is certainly not she, but I. Let her know that I desire only one thing—freedom from her," he wrote in a letter to one of his children.

One night, Tolstoy abruptly left his hut for good. In a note addressed to his wife of forty-eight years, he wrote, "I am doing what people of my age very often do . . . giving up the world, in order to spend my last days alone and in silence. . . . I do not think that I have left home because I do not love you. I love and pity you with all my heart, but I cannot do otherwise than I am doing." Tolstoy, already in ill health, died in a railroad station ten days after leaving home. Far from being "alone and in silence," he was flanked by hundreds of onlookers, journalists, a film crew, and his wife. "Forgive me, forgive me!" she told him beside his death bench. "I have never loved anyone but you."

IN HIS OWN WORDS
The Honeymoon's Over

Tolstoy's wife Sophia transcribed his novel *The Kreutzer Sonata* by hand. This task was assuredly uncomfortable for her because of the ways in which the details mirrored her marriage to Tolstoy:

> Cold hostility was our normal state. . . . We had spats about the coffee, the tablecloth, the carriage, games of cards—trifles, in short, which could not be of the least importance to either of us. . . .

All husbands who live the married life that I lived must either resort to outside debauchery, or separate from their wives, or kill themselves, or kill their wives. . . .

Timeline

350 BC   Diogenes the Cynic, believing that "what is natural cannot be wrong," farts, urinates, defecates, and masturbates in public. Men are amused, women are horrified.

60 BC   Titus Lucretius ingests a love potion, which drives him insane.

41   Seneca the Younger is banished from Rome for sleeping with a married Roman princess.

385   Saint Augustine of Hippo ends his engagement to a ten-year-old girl after a heavenly voice persuades him to lead a life of celibacy.

1118   Peter Abelard abandons his wife Héloïse to a convent so that he can spend more time on his studies. Her protective uncle castrates him.

1250   Saint Thomas Aquinas's family hires a prostitute to seduce him. Aquinas chases her away with a hot firebrand.

1540   John Calvin's engagement to a young German-speaking woman is called off when she fails to learn French.

1634 René Descartes has sex with a maid, fathering an illegitimate child. It is the first and last time he ever has sex.

1766 Nicolas Chamfort contracts a venereal disease that scars his good looks and disfigures his genitals beyond repair.

1768 Jean-Jacques Rousseau personally abandons all five of his newborns to a hospital for unwanted children.

1774 Johann Wolfgang von Goethe publishes *The Sorrows of Young Werther*, a tragic romance novel that causes dozens of young and heartbroken European men to commit suicide.

1784 Denis Diderot's wife burns love letters that her husband wrote to and received from his mistress Sophie Volland.

1800 Georg Wilhelm Friedrich Hegel fathers an illegitimate child with his landlord's wife. Hegel leaves town rather quickly.

1818 Arthur Schopenhauer fathers a child with a maid in Dresden during a single night of passion.

1826 Auguste Comte throws knives at his wife and slits his own throat at the dinner table during a mental breakdown. His wife, tired of his moody antics, finally leaves him sixteen years later.

1840 Henry David Thoreau's marriage proposal to Ellen Sewall is rejected. He gives up on love forever.

1841 Søren Kierkegaard breaks up with his fiancée of thirteen months, Regine Olsen, to spare her from his existential angst.

1862 Leo Tolstoy shows his diaries to his bride on their wedding day, revealing his world of prostitutes, promiscuity, gonorrhea, and homoerotic thoughts in unflinching detail.

1868 Fyodor Dostoyevsky pawns his wife's wedding ring to pay down his gambling debts. She eventually gets it back.

1872 Henry Ward Beecher, the most famous minister in America, is tried for adultery. He refuses to place his hand on the Bible and swear under oath, sealing his guilt in the court of public opinion.

1889 Friedrich Nietzsche has a severe psychotic breakdown and never regains his sanity. He dies in 1900 from complications of syphilis.

1895 On his deathbed, Friedrich Engels reveals that his suspected son was actually fathered by his friend and collaborator Karl Marx.

1921 Bertrand Russell divorces his first wife.

1928 Jean-Paul Sartre's engagement to Germaine Marron is broken by her parents after he fails his teaching exam. It doesn't bother Sartre much, as he has been sleeping with actress Simone Jollivet.

1933 Martin Heidegger joins the Nazi Party, despite the fact that his mistress Hannah Arendt is Jewish. She hightails it to America.

1935 Bertrand Russell divorces his second wife.

1942 Albert Camus divorces his first wife Simone Hié after discovering that she has been having sex with a doctor in exchange for morphine.

1952   Bertrand Russell divorces his third wife.

1952   John Dewey dies alone after his second wife alienates his family and friends.

1955   Ayn Rand begins an extramarital affair with student Nathaniel Branden, who is twenty-five years her junior.

1980   Simone de Beauvoir adopts her lesbian lover Sylvie Le Bon as her daughter.

1980   Louis Althusser "accidentally" strangles his wife in her sleep. He spends less than three years in an institution before being released back into society.

Acknowledgments

Thank you to my agent, Brandi Bowles, for pulling me out of the slush pile.

Thank you to Stephanie Meyers. This was truly a collaborative effort and I consider myself lucky to have found such a talented editor.

Thank you to my readers Tiffany Jensen, Jason Walter, and Joseph Leman for your feedback and close reading.

Thank you to my parents and grandparents who, along with Huey Lewis, taught me about the Power of Love.

And, of course, a special thanks to my wife, Gwendolyn Lee, who didn't flinch when I asked permission to write a book on the pitfalls of romantic love while we were on our Alaskan honeymoon cruise.

Selected Bibliography

GENERAL WORKS

Botton, Alain de. *The Consolations of Philosophy*. New York: Pantheon Books, 2000.

Cohen, Martin. *Philosophical Tales*. Oxford: Blackwell Publishing, 2008.

Critchley, Simon. *The Book of Dead Philosophers*. London: Granta, 2008.

Soble, Alan, ed. *Eros, Agape, and Philia: Readings in the Philosophy of Love*. New York: Paragon Press, 1989.

————. *The Philosophy of Sex and Love: An Introduction*. St. Paul, MN: Paragon Press, 2008.

————. *Sex from Plato to Paglia*. Westport, CT: Greenwood Press, 2006.

Solomon, Robert C., ed. *The Philosophy of (Erotic) Love*. Lawrence, KS: University Press of Kansas, 1991.

Introduction

No Direction Home. Interview with Bob Dylan. Director Martin Scorsese. DVD. Paramount, 2005.

Pollack, Neal. Introduction. *Love Is a Four-Letter Word: True Stories of Breakups, Bad Relationships, and Broken Hearts*. Edited by Michael Taeckens. New York: Plume, 2009.

BY PHILOSOPHER

Peter Abelard

Abélard, Peter. *The Story of My Misfortunes: An Autobiography*. St. Paul, MN: T. A. Boyd, 1922.

Abélard, Peter, and Héloïse d'Argenteuil. *The Love Letters of Abélard and Heloise, Translated from the Original Latin and Now Reprinted from the Edition of 1722: Together with a Brief Account of Their Lives and Work*. Indianapolis: The Bobbs-Merrill Company, 1903.

Clanchy, M. T. *Abélard: A Medieval Life*. Oxford: Wiley-Blackwell, 1999.

Mews, Constant J. *Abélard and Heloise*. New York: Oxford University Press, 2005.

Louis Althusser

Althusser, Louis. *The Future Lasts Forever*. Edited by Olivier Corpet and Yann Moulier Bougtang. Translated by Richard Veasey. New York: New Press, 1993.

Davis, Colin. "Historical Reason and Autobiographical Folly in Sartre and Althusser." *Sartre Studies International* 10, no. 1 (2004): 1ff.

Ferretter, Luke. *Louis Althusser.* New York: Routledge, 2006.

Saint Thomas Aquinas

Chesterton, G. K. "St. Thomas Aquinas." *The Spectator*, February 27, 1932.

Aristotle

Aristotle. *The Works of Aristotle: The Famous Philosopher.* Translated by William Salmon. London: J. Coker & Co., c. 1900.

Mayhew, Robert. *The Female in Aristotle's Biology.* Chicago: The University of Chicago Press, 2004.

Price, A. W. *Love and Friendship in Plato and Aristotle.* Oxford: Clarendon Press, 1990.

Russell, Bertrand. *The History of Western Philosophy and Its Connection with Political and Social Circumstances from the Earliest Times to the Present Day.* London: G. Allen and Unwin Ltd., 1946.

Saint Augustine of Hippo

Augustine, Saint. *The City of God.* Translated by Marcus D. D. Dods. New York: Modern Library, 1950.

———. *Confessions.* Translated by Edward Bouverie Pusey. New York: E. P. Dutton & Co., 1907.

Simone de Beauvoir

Beauvoir, Simone de. *The Prime of Life.* Translated by Peter Green. Cleveland: World Pub. Co., 1962.

Fullbrook, Kate, and Edward Fullbrook. *Simone de Beauvoir and*

Jean-Paul Sartre: The Remaking of a Twentieth-Century Legend. New York: Basic Books, 1994.

Rowley, Hazel. *Tête-à-Tête: Simone de Beauvoir and Jean-Paul Sartre.* New York: HarperCollins, 2005.

Henry Ward Beecher

Ellis, Dr. John B. *Free Love and Its Votaries; or, American Socialism Unmasked.* San Francisco: A. L. Bancroft & Co., 1870.

Shaplen, Robert. *Free Love and Heavenly Sinners.* New York: Knopf, 1954.

Woodhull, Victoria C. "And the Truth Shall Make You Free: A Speech on the Principles of Social Freedom." November 20, 1871.

John Calvin

Bouwsma, W. J. *John Calvin: A Sixteenth-Century Portrait.* New York: Oxford University Press, 1989.

Selderhuis, Herman J. *John Calvin: A Pilgrim's Life.* Downers Grove, IL: IVP Academic, 2009.

Witte, John, Jr. "Between Sacrament and Contract: Marriage as Covenant in John Calvin's Geneva," *Calvin Handbook.* Edited by Herman Selderhuis. Translated by Henry J. Baron et al. Cambridge: Wm. B. Eeardmans Publishing Co., 2009.

Albert Camus

Camus, Albert. *The Stranger.* Translated by Matthew Ward. New York: Random House, 1989.

Thorpe, Vanessa. "Charting the Amazing Love Life of the Amorous Existentialist." *The Independent*, October 12, 1997.

Todd, Olivier. *Albert Camus: A Life*. Cambridge: Da Capo Press, 2000.

Nicolas Chamfort

Arnaud, Claude. *Chamfort: A Biography*. Translated by Deke Dusinberre. Chicago: University of Chicago Press, 1992.

Chamfort, Nicolas de. *The Cynic's Breviary: Maxims and Anecdotes*. Translated by Sebastien Roch. London: E. Mathews, 1902.

Auguste Comte

Comte, Auguste. *Passages from the Letters of Auguste Comte*. Translated by John Kells Ingram. London: A. & C. Black, 1901.

Pickering, Mary. *Auguste Comte: An Intellectual Biography*. New York: Cambridge University Press, 1993.

Thompson, Kenneth. *Auguste Comte: The Foundation of Sociology*. New York: Wiley, 1975.

René Descartes

Descartes, René. *Passions of the Soul*. Translated by Stephen Voss. Indianapolis: Hackett Publishing Co., 1989.

"Descartes' Life and Works." *Stanford Encyclopedia of Philosophy*. February 27, 2007. plato.stanford.edu/entries/descartes-works. Retrieved on October 14, 2009.

Gaukroger, S. *Descartes: An Intellectual Biography*. Oxford: Clarendon Press, 1997.

Grayling, A. C. *Descartes: The Life of René Descartes and Its Place in His Times*. London: Free Press, 2005.

John Dewey

Dewey, John. *Human Nature and Conduct: An Introduction to Social Psychology*. New York: Holt, 1922.

———. *The Poems of John Dewey*. Edited by Jo Ann Boydston. Carbondale: Southern Illinois University Press, 1977.

Rockefeller, Steven C. *John Dewey: Religious Faith and Democratic Humanism*. New York: Columbia University Press, 1991.

Ryan, Alan. *John Dewey and the High Tide of American Liberalism*. New York: W. W. Norton, 1995.

Walker, Linda Robinson. "John Dewey at Michigan." *Michigan Today* 29, no. 2 (Summer 1997).

Westbrook, Robert B. *John Dewey and American Democracy*. Ithaca, NY: Cornell University Press, 1991.

Denis Diderot

Hall, Evelyn Beatrice. *The Friends of Voltaire*. London: Smith Elder and Co., 1906.

Diogenes the Cynic

Laertius, Diogenes. *The Lives and Opinions of Eminent Philosophers*. Translated by C. D. Yonge. London: H. G. Bohn, 1853.

Fyodor Dostoyevsky

Dostoyevsky, Fyodor. *Letters of Fyodor Michailovitch Dostoevsky to His Family and Friends*. Translated by Ethel Colburn Mayne. New York: The Macmillan Company, 1914.

Frank, Joseph. *Dostoevsky: The Miraculous Years, 1865–1871*. Princeton, NJ: Princeton University Press, 1995.

Lantz, Kenneth. *The Dostoevsky Encyclopedia*. Westport, CT: Greenwood Press, 2004.

Friedrich Engels

Carver, Terrell. "Marx's 'Illegitimate Son' or Gresham's Law in the World of Scholarship. Marx Myths.org. marxmyths.org/terrell-carver/article.htm. Retrieved on October 14, 2009.

Engels, Friedrich. "Helene Demuth Obituary." *The People's Press*, November 22, 1890.

————. *The Origin of the Family, Private Property and the State*. New York: International Publishers, 1942.

Green, John. *Engels: A Revolutionary Life*. London: Artery Publications, 2008.

Hunt, Tristam. *The Frock-Coated Communist: The Revolutionary Life of Friedrich Engels*. London: Allen Lane/Penguin Books UK, 2009.

Marx, Karl, and Friedrich Engels. *Manifesto of the Communist Party*. New York: Socialist Literature Co., 1912.

Johann Wolfgang von Goethe

Bates, Alfred, ed. "Goethe's Love Affairs." *The Drama: Its History, Literature and Influence on Civilization*, Vol. 11. London: Historical Publishing Company, 1906: 66–69.

Goethe, Johann Wolfgang von. *The Autobiography of Goethe*. Translated by John Oxenford and A. J. W. Morrison. London: Bell & Daldy, 1872.

————. *Sorrows of Young Werther, Elective Affinities*. Translated by R. D. Boylan. Edited by Nathan Haskell Dole. Boston: F. A. Nicolls & Company, 1902.

Marsen, Paul. "Operationalising Memetics—Suicide, the Werther Effect, and the Work of David P. Phillips." University of Sussex. pespmc1.vub.ac.be/conf/memepap/marsden.html. Retrieved on October 14, 2009.

Siebers, T. "The Werther Effect: The Esthetics of Suicide." *Mosaic* (Winnipeg) 26, no. 1 (1993): 15ff.

Georg Wilhelm Friedrich Hegel

Harris, Henry Silton. *Hegel's Development: Toward the Sunlight, 1770–1801.* Oxford: Clarendon Press, 1972.

Hegel, Georg Wilhelm Friedrich. *The Logic of Hegel, Translated from the Encyclopaedia of the Philosophical Sciences.* Translated by W. Wallace. Oxford: Clarendon Press, 1892.

———. *The Philosophy of Right.* Translated by S. W. Dyde. New York: Dover, 2005: 87.

Pinkard, Terry. *Hegel: A Biography.* New York: Cambridge University Press, 2000.

Martin Heidegger

Ettinger, Elzbieta. *Hannah Arendt/Martin Heidegger.* New Haven: Yale University Press, 1995.

Honan, William H. "Book on Philosopher's Life Stirs Scholarly Debate Over Her Legacy." *New York Times*, November 5, 1995.

David Hume

Hume, David. *The Philosophical Works of David Hume.* Edinburgh: A. Black and W. Tait, 1826.

————. *The Philosophy of David Hume*. Edited by V. C. Chappell. New York: Modern Library, 1963.

Immanuel Kant

Jaspers, K. *Kant*. Edited by Hannah Arendt. Translated by R. Manheim. San Diego, CA: Harcourt Brace Jovanovich, 1962.

Quincey, Thomas de. *Essays in Philosophy*. New York: Hurd and Houghton, 1877.

Schott, Robin May, ed. *Feminist Interpretations of Immanuel Kant*. University Park, PA: Pennsylvania State University Press, 1997.

Soble, Alan. "Kant and Sexual Perversion." *The Monist* 86, no. 1 (2003), 55ff.

Søren Kierkegaard

Hall, R. L. *The Human Embrace: The Love of Philosophy and the Philosophy of Love: Kierkegaard, Cavell, Nussbaum*. University Park, PA: Pennsylvania State University Press, 2000.

Hannay, A. *Kierkegaard: A Biography*. Cambridge, England: Cambridge University Press, 2001.

Updike, John. "Not a Seducer." *The New York Review of Books* 44, no. 14 (September 25, 1997).

John Locke

Glausser, W. *Locke and Blake: A Conversation Across the Eighteenth Century*. Gainesville, FL: University Press of Florida, 1998.

Pfeffer, Jacqueline L. "The Family in John Locke's Political Thought." *Polity* 33 (2001).

Titus Lucretius

Bounia, Alexandria. *The Nature of Classical Collecting: Collectors and Collections, 100 BCE–100 CE*. Aldershot, England: Ashgate Publishing, Limited, 2004.

Hirsch, Dr. A. R., and J. J. Gruss. "Human Male Sexual Response to Olfactory Stimuli." *J. Neurol. Orthop. Med. Surg* 19 (1999): 14–19.

Lucretius, Titus. *The Way Things Are*. Translated by Rolfe Humphries. Bloomington: Indiana University Press, 1968.

Tennyson, Alfred. "Lucretius." *Every Saturday*, May 2, 1868: 576.

Friedrich Nietzsche

Mencken, H. L. *The Philosophy of Friedrich Nietzsche*. Boston: Luce and Company, 1908.

Moore, G. *Nietzsche, Biology, and Metaphor*. Cambridge, England: Cambridge University Press, 2002.

Nietzsche, Friedrich. *Selected Letters of Friedrich Nietzsche*. Edited by Oscar Ley. Translated by Anthony Mario Ludovici. Garden City, NY: Doubleday, Page & Company, 1921.

Plato

Plato. *Plato: Phaedrus, Ion, Gorgias, and Symposium, with Passages from the Republic and Laws*. Translated by L. Cooper. London: Oxford University Press, 1938.

Price, A. W. *Love and Friendship in Plato and Aristotle*. Oxford: Clarendon Press, 1990.

Ayn Rand

Branden, Nathaniel. *My Years with Ayn Rand*. San Francisco: Jossey-Bass, 1999.

Honan, William H. "Book on Philosopher's Life Stirs Scholarly Debate Over Her Legacy." *New York Times*, November 5, 1995.

Rand, Ayn. *Fountainhead*. Philadelphia: The Blakiston Company, 1943.

Toffler, Alvin. "*Playboy* Interview: Ayn Rand." *Playboy*, March 1964.

Jean-Jacques Rousseau

Rousseau, Jean-Jacques. *The Confessions of Jean-Jacques Rousseau*. Translated by J. M. Cohen. London: Penguin Books, 1953.

————. *Discourse on the Origin of Inequality*. Translated by Donald A. Cress. Indianapolis: Hackett Publishing Co., 1992.

————. *Emile, or Education Book 3*. Translated by Ossian Herbert Lang. New York and Chicago: E. L. Kellogg & Co., 1893.

————. *The Social Contract; or, Principles of Political Right* (2nd ed.). Translated by Henry John Tozer. New York: Charles Scribner's Sons, 1898.

Bertrand Russell

Monk, Ray. *Bertrand Russell: The Ghost of Madness, 1921–1970*. New York: Free Press, 2001.

Russell, Bertrand. *The Autobiography of Bertrand Russell*. Boston: Little, Brown, 1967.

―――. *The Basic Writings of Bertrand Russell, 1903–1959*. Edited by R. E. Egner and L. E. Dennon. New York: Simon and Schuster, 1961.

―――. *Marriage and Morals*. New York: Liveright, 1970.

Jean-Paul Sartre

Davis, C. "Historical Reason and Autobiographical Folly in Sartre and Althusser." *Sartre Studies International* 10, no. 1 (2004): 1ff.

Gerassi, John. *Talking with Sartre: Conversations and Debates*. New Haven, CT: Yale University Press, 2009.

Rowley, Hazel. *Tête-à-Tête: Simone de Beauvoir and Jean-Paul Sartre*. New York: HarperCollins, 2005.

Sartre by Himself. Directors Alexandre Astruc and Michel Contat. Interview with Jean-Paul Sartre. VHS. Interama Video Classics: 1989.

Sartre, Jean-Paul. *Being and Nothingness*. Translated by Hazel E. Barnes. New York: Gramercy Books, 1994.

Wyatt, J. "The Impossible Project of Love in Sartre's 'Being and Nothingness,' Dirty Hands and the Room." *Sartre Studies International* 12, no. 2 (2006): 1ff.

Arthur Schopenhauer

Schopenhauer, Arthur. *Essays of Schopenhauer*. New York: The Walter Scott Publishing Co., Ltd., 1897.

Seneca the Younger

Griffin, M. T. *Seneca: A Philosopher in Politics*. Oxford: Clarendon Press, 1992.

Seneca, Lucius Annaeus. *Ad Lucillum Epistulae Morales*. Translated by Richard M. Gummere. New York: G. P. Putnam's Sons, 1918.

———. *On Benefits*. Translated by Aubrey Stewart. London: George Bell and Sons, 1887.

Tacitus. *The Annals*. Translated by Alfred John Church and William Jackson Brodribb. London: Macmillan and Co., 1876.

Socrates

Plato. *Plato: Phaedrus, Ion, Gorgias, and Symposium, with Passages from the Republic and Laws*. Translated by L. Cooper. London: Oxford University Press, 1938.

Emanuel Swedenborg

Swedenborg, Emanuel. *The Delights of Wisdom Pertaining to Conjugal Love: After Which Follow the Pleasures of Insanity Pertaining to Promiscuous Love*. Translated by Samuel M. Warren. Edited by Louis H. Tafel. West Chester, PA: Swedenborg Foundation, 1998.

———. *Swedenborg's Journal of Dreams, 1743–1744*. Edited by G. E. Klemming and William Ross Woofenden. Translated by J. J. G. Wilkinson. New York: Swedenborg Foundation, 1977.

Toksvig, Signe. *Emanuel Swedenborg: Scientist and Mystic*. New Haven, CT: Yale University Press, 1948.

Henry David Thoreau

Collias, Nicholas. "It's In for Historical Revisionists to Out." *Boise Weekly*, June 2, 2004.

Harding, Walter. *The Days of Henry Thoreau: A Biography*. Princeton, NJ: Princeton University Press, 1982.

―――. "Thoreau's Sexuality." *The Journal of Homosexuality* 21, no. 3 (1991): 23–45.

Thoreau, Henry David. *The Writings of Henry David Thoreau*. Edited by Michael Meyer. New York: AMS Press, 1982.

Leo Tolstoy

Bunin, Ivan Alekseevich. *The Liberation of Tolstoy: A Tale of Two Writers*. Translated and edited by Thomas Gaiton. Evanston, IL: Northwestern University Press, 2001.

Tolstoy, Leo. *The Diaries of Leo Tolstoy*. Translated by Lev Nikolaevich. New York: E. P. Dutton & Company, 1917.

―――. *The Kreutzer Sonata*. Translated by Benjamin R. Tucker. Boston: B. R. Tucker, 1890.

Wilson, A. N. *Tolstoy*. New York: Norton, 1988.